Time to Change

Time to Change

An Ignatian Retreat
In Daily Life

MICHAEL
CAMPBELL-JOHNSTON SJ

DARTON·LONGMAN+TODD

First published in 2010 by
Darton, Longman and Todd Ltd
1 Spencer Court
140 – 142 Wandsworth High Street
London SW18 4JJ

ISBN 978-0-232-52782-7

A catalogue record for this book is available from
the British Library.

Designed by Judy Linard
Set in 10.5/12.5pt Bembo and News Gothic Demi
Printed and bound in Great Britain by
Thomson Litho, East Kilbride, Scotland

Contents

Introductory Note

The pages that follow were originally composed to be recorded for use with a MP3 or portable media player. This is why they are addressed, especially at the outset, to the person supposedly listening to them. The welcome can, however, easily be extended to a person who is reading them. But now that they are printed in book form and made available on a website (see Endnotes), it should be remembered they constitute a document not intended to be read, but rather to be 'done' or 'made'. They consist in directions or suggestions for a retreat which can only be properly assessed once the retreat has been made. This entails specific conditions, the most important of which are described on days 2 and 3.

The same is true of the little book on which this is based: the *Spiritual Exercises* of St Ignatius. It is recounted how Aldous Huxley once picked this up, flipped through it, and declared it drab, trite and uninspiring. The reason is the same: the Exercises are not meant to be read, but to be made in silence before God, usually and ideally with the help of a director or guide. This is why, in his lifetime, Ignatius resisted their publication. Only one edition appeared, a Latin translation made by a French colleague from a Spanish original, and only 500 copies were printed, which Ignatius was very loath to distribute.

The value of this present document therefore depends on making the retreat it advocates. And this commitment, as St Ignatius points out, should be undertaken with 'a magnanimous spirit and with great liberality towards one's

Creator and Lord' (Annotation 5). A prior disposition is therefore required.

But this does not mean the Spiritual Exercises should be restricted to Roman Catholics or, at least, to already practising Christians. St Ignatius described them as a means for 'the overcoming of self and the ordering of one's life on the basis of a decision made in freedom from any ill-ordered attachments'. Such an aim can be pursued by someone of any religious creed or none at all. Jerome Nadal, who was his secretary, on being asked for whom the Spiritual Exercises were suited, answered: 'For Catholics, for Protestants and for pagans.'

My hope and prayer is that this simple presentation of the Spiritual Exercises of St Ignatius will be of benefit not only to those already well acquainted with them, but also to a large number of people, whatever their religious beliefs, who would not ordinarily have access to Ignatian spirituality.

Michael Campbell-Johnston SJ
Barbados
January 2009

Day 1: Why a Retreat?

Good morning, good afternoon, good evening, good night!

I don't know what time of the day (or night) it is for you who are reading this, but I want to start by saying 'hello' to you, by welcoming you to this retreat in daily life and by introducing myself.

I am a Roman Catholic priest and I belong to a religious congregation called the 'Society of Jesus'. It was founded some 450 years ago by St Ignatius of Loyola, a Spanish gentleman who changed his life from being the soldier of an earthly king to becoming one of the King of Heaven. So I am a Jesuit priest. I am called CJ, because my full surname is such a mouthful.

I was born in England but a large part of my life has been spent in Latin America doing missionary work of various types. I am now living on the island of Barbados from where I am speaking to you. I look after a small parish devoted to St Francis of Assisi. I also run a small guest house for fellow Jesuits from Guyana who come here to make a retreat or have a holiday. The house is right on the sea and has a beautiful view over the blue Caribbean.

To be honest, it is partly a semi-retirement job since neither occupation, guest-master or parish priest, is too demanding and I am now 76 years old. I have extra time to spare, and spend part of it writing, doing translation work and sometimes giving retreats.

So there you have me! I wish you could now give

me your introduction for I would like to know you better, but no one has yet invented a two-way system between an author and his or her readers. Perhaps that will come one day.

But though I don't know your name, or what you look like, or what you do, there is one thing I do know about you: you are interested in making a retreat in your daily life. For that is why you are reading this book and that is what I shall be trying to help you to do: to make a retreat, spread over perhaps some 30 days, though there is no time limit and it can last for as long as you find helpful. And the idea is to make it without interrupting too much your ordinary daily life and all the things you have to do.

So perhaps a few words at the start about a retreat. What is it? Why is it important? What will it involve you in?

I suppose the most important thing about a retreat is that it is an attempt to see beyond the 101 cares and occupations you normally have and to ask yourself where it is all leading. What's the purpose of it all? Do you remember the gospel scene when Jesus met with the two sisters, Martha and Mary? Martha was busy with all the housework and looking after the visitors. She complained to Jesus that Mary was doing nothing to help her but just sitting there listening to him. Jesus replied to her: 'Martha, Martha, you worry and fret about so many things, and yet few are needed, indeed only one.' And then he added something that must have annoyed her greatly: 'It is Mary who has chosen the better part; it is not to be taken from her.'

It is a very simple story with a clear meaning. I suggest you use it in your prayer today. If it helps, you can imagine being there yourself, either as Mary or Martha.

To make a retreat is to choose Mary's part. For a short time, you try to stop worrying and fretting about so many different things, and sit in silence at God's feet, so to speak, just to listen. And you want to try and understand better what Jesus means when he says: 'Only one thing is needed.' What is that one thing? Where can I find it? What effect should it have on my daily occupations and cares?

In case you don't have a Bible with you, I will end by inserting here the short passage that comes from Luke 10:38–42. However, if you could have a New Testament or Bible at hand during your prayer, it would be helpful, though not essential.

> In the course of their journey he came to a village, and a woman named Martha welcomed him into her house. She had a sister called Mary, who sat down at the Lord's feet and listened to him speaking. Now Martha who was distracted with all the serving said, 'Lord, do you not care that my sister is leaving me to do the serving all by myself? Please tell her to help me.' But the Lord answered: 'Martha, Martha,' he said 'you worry and fret about so many things, and yet few are needed, indeed only one. It is Mary who has chosen the better part; it is not to be taken from her.'

Notes

Day 2: God is Calling You

Yesterday we reflected, you and I, on Martha's sister Mary, who, Jesus said, had chosen the better part because, unlike Martha, she had put aside her worrying and fretting about many things, so as to concentrate on the one thing that is needed.

And we saw that this is exactly what a retreat invites us to do. Professional religious, priests and sisters, normally do this each year for eight days or so. They often go away to a special house (retreat house), having left behind their jobs, their daily worries and cares, their computers and mobile phones, so as to be in silence and listen more easily to the voice of the Lord.

Most of you can't do this because you have your families and jobs to care for. You can't easily get away and escape, even if you could afford to do so. This is precisely why a retreat in daily life was invented. You attempt to make a retreat while carrying on with your ordinary occupations, the only difference being giving up half an hour or an hour each day to spend it in God's presence.

This is absolutely essential because the person who gives the retreat is not the retreat director, if you have one, nor is it the writer of this book. It is none other than God. So the first thing you have to do is to make an act of faith that God really has something to say to you at this particular moment in your life. You must ask God to speak to you and help you to understand more clearly what you are being called to do. This is what a retreat is for.

God is calling you by name just as he called the

prophets in the Old Testament or Jesus called his disciples in the New. And you should reply as they did.

- God put Abraham to the test. 'Abraham, Abraham' he called. 'Here I am' he replied. (Genesis 22:1)
- The angel of Yahweh called to him from heaven. 'Abraham. Abraham' he said. 'I am here' he replied. (Genesis 22:11)
- God called to him from the middle of the bush. 'Moses, Moses' he said. 'Here I am' he answered. (Exodus 3:1–4)
- Yahweh then came and stood by, calling as he had done before, 'Samuel! Samuel!' Samuel answered, 'Speak, Yahweh, your servant is listening.' (I Samuel 3:10)
- The Angel went in and said to her, 'Rejoice, so highly favoured! The Lord is with you.' She was deeply disturbed by these words and asked herself what this greeting could mean . . . 'I am the handmaid of the Lord,' said Mary, 'let what you have said be done to me.' (Luke 1:28 and 38)
- As Jesus was walking on from there, he saw a man named Matthew sitting by the customs house, and he said to him, 'Follow me'. And he got up and followed him. (Matthew 9:9)

But to hear God calling, you have to listen and this is not always so easy. There is normally so much noise in our lives today. I am not thinking only of people talking all the time, or the radio and television blaring, not to mention mobile phones or other contraptions. But our minds are full of ideas and thoughts that we also need to silence if we are to hear God. So it is not just cutting out our daily lives for a few moments, but also trying to find a real inner silence in our minds so that God can take them over.

This is what true prayer is and it is sometimes called 'the prayer of silence'. It means not using words or formulas, or even ideas or imaginations, but just being in God's presence. You may remember the wonderful example given by the Curé of Ars who asked an illiterate peasant what he did during the hours he spent on his knees before the Blessed Sacrament. He replied: 'I look at God and God looks at me.' Or the journalist who asked Mother Teresa: 'When you pray, what do you say to God?' She replied: 'I don't say anything. I listen.' The journalist: 'All right. What then does God say to you?' She replied: 'God doesn't say anything. God listens.' And then she added: 'If you can't understand that, I can't explain it to you.'

Try to do this today in your prayer. Hear God calling you by name, and reply 'Here I am', 'Speak Lord, your servant is listening.' And then listen to the Lord. This is where I stop talking too, to give God a chance.

Notes

Day 3: Be Still and Know that I Am God

Yesterday you looked at what a retreat is for and I hope it became clear that it is basically to answer a call from God. God is calling you by name at this particular moment of your life because there is something important to say to you. This means that a retreat is not mainly something that you do, but something that God does within you. Your job is to make this possible, in other words to take the necessary steps that will allow God to speak and you to listen.

Some of these are simple practical things such as finding a place and time where you can be alone without interruption and in silence. You should have already decided how much time you can put aside each day. Be as generous as you can in this, but don't attempt something impossible that you know you won't be able to fulfil. The crucial thing is to really keep to what you decide. You can always seek advice on this from a friend or counsellor. It is also highly desirable to have a brief reflection period each day, separate from your prayer time, to consider how your prayer time has gone and to jot down some notes about what impressed you or where you had difficulties. The blank areas in this booklet can be used for this. There is one for each of the thirty days. These should be shared with someone who knows you well and has experience of spiritual things so that they can guide and encourage you.

In a more traditional retreat, this is the sort of practical help the retreat giver or director can give to the retreatant. Unfortunately I can't do any of these things for you in person. You will have to make your own decisions in accordance with your possibilities and particular situation, seeking advice, if possible, from someone you trust. But you should remember that you are not doing this primarily for yourself, but to answer God who is calling you by name.

This is summed up very well in a short verse of Psalm 46 that not only explains what a retreat is for but also indicates how to set about making one. The verse is: BE STILL, AND KNOW THAT I AM GOD (Psalm 46:11).

We have already said something about being still and know that it is not so easy to achieve. Bodily stillness for most people is relatively easy. To pray we need to put ourselves in a comfortable position, sitting or lying or whatever, and then, with the body at rest, not to move. It could be that a lying position might encourage sleep, in which case, a sitting position should be chosen.

But, as you may remember, it is the mental stillness that sometimes costs us most, that inner silence where our thoughts are not chasing each other pell-mell around our brains. Sometimes we have to make a deliberate effort to let go of them, by concentrating on something different such as our mere breathing in or out.

For it is only in this inner peace and silence, this stillness, that we will come to appreciate more the second part of that verse from the psalm: KNOW THAT I AM GOD.

This knowledge of God is something we will be trying to deepen and increase throughout the retreat. But it cannot come from me or you. It can only come from God when we are still. As one retreat giver has put it very well: 'To seek God means first of all to let yourself be found by Him.'

This then is your task in your prayer today: to let

yourself be found by God. To help you in this, I give you three brief passages from the prophet Isaiah that I have found very helpful. I hope you will be helped by them too.

Do not be afraid, for I have redeemed you;
I have called you by your name, you are mine.
Should you pass through the sea, I will be with you;
Or through rivers, they will not swallow you up.
Should you walk through fire, you will not be
    scorched
and the flames will not burn you.
For I am Yahweh, your God,
the Holy One of Israel, your saviour. (43:1–6)

Listen to me, House of Jacob,
all you who remain of the House of Israel,
you who have been carried since birth,
whom I have carried since the time you were born.
In your old age I shall be still the same,
When your hair is grey I shall still support you.
I have already done so, I have carried you,
I shall still support and deliver you. (46:3–4)

Does a woman forget her baby at the breast,
Or fail to cherish the son of her womb?
Yet even if these forget,
I will never forget you. (49:15)

Notes

Day 4: God Is Love

You have considered more than once that in and through this retreat God is calling you and that this is the most important part of it. You are probably not sure *how* he will do it and may be a little worried that you might miss his call, or even that there may not be one. But don't lose hope. Be sure that somehow or other a call or sign will come.

How can you be so sure about this, you may ask. Well, we can find an answer if we reflect on *why* God is calling. And this is what I want to propose for your consideration and prayer today. The answer is really very simple but at the same time very profound. God is calling you for the simple reason that God is love and you are part of that love.

Our Lord himself explained this to his disciples during the last supper, the final occasion he would have a chance of talking to them all together. As St John recounts in his gospel, he put his reasons in a prayer addressed to his Father:

'Father, I want those you have given me to be with me where I am, so that they may always see the glory you have given me because you loved me before the foundation of the world. Father, Righteous One, the world has not known you, but I have known you, and these have known that you have sent me. I have made your name known to them and will continue to make it known, so that the love with which you loved me may be in them, and so that I may be in them.' (John 17:24–26)

These are tremendous and almost unbelievable words. And, when Our Lord says I 'will continue to make it known', it is clear he is addressing not only the disciples but all who come after them, that is you and me. So to share in God's love is your destiny, my destiny and the destiny of us all. It is the only real explanation of our lives, since it is the reason for our existence and the existence of the whole of creation.

Once again it is St John who explains this in his first epistle in words which are well known but excite wonder every time we reflect on them:

My dear people, let us love one another since love comes from God and everyone who loves is begotten by God and knows God. Anyone who fails to love can never have known God, because God is love. (1 John 4:7–8)

So the very essence of God's nature, which is a mystery since we cannot fully understand it, is not a mystery of isolation or individualism but of sharing, of mutual outpouring, of giving and receiving. This is why, as Jesus taught, though God is one, God is a trinity of three persons each equal to the other. The exchange of love between Father and Son is what he called the Holy Spirit, the spirit of love. And it is because of this love that everything, you, me and all else, exists. As St John says again, 'Anyone who lives in love lives in God, and God lives in him' (1 John 4:16).

The old scholastic philosophers used to say: 'Bonum est diffusivum sui', which I am sure you have already translated as: 'The nature of goodness is the outpouring of self'. In other words, the principle and foundation of all that exists comes directly from the relationship of giving and receiving which is the essence of the Trinity.

This must all seem very abstract and possibly remote to you. But, as I hope you will see soon, it is in fact very down to earth with practical and concrete consequences. But before looking at these, I want to refer to a modern scientist who not only agreed with what St John says above but declared that love is the fundamental law of the universe, the prime and indispensable motor of its progress. His name is Teilhard de Chardin, a French Jesuit who lived and died in the last century and was a palaeontologist, that is, an expert on fossils and the earth's history.

This is what he wrote:

> Love has always been carefully eliminated from the realist and positivist concepts of the world, but sooner or later we will have to acknowledge that it is the fundamental impulse of life or, if you prefer, the one natural medium in which the rising course of evolution can proceed. With love omitted, there is truly nothing ahead of us except the forbidding prospect of standardisation and enslavement; the doom of ants and termites. It is through love and within love that we must look for the deepening of our deepest self, in the life-giving coming together of humankind. (*The Future of Man*, p. 57)

So Teilhard's call is not all that different from that of St John: he says:

> Love one another, recognising in the heart of each of you the same God who is being born. Those words,

first spoken two thousand years ago, now begin to reveal themselves as the essential structural law of what we call progress and evolution. They enter the scientific field of cosmic energy and its necessary laws. (pp. 78–9)

This is a quite remarkable statement from a highly competent professional scientist!

I would like to suggest for your prayer and reflection today the texts I have quoted from St John and Teilhard de Chardin. You should ask God to help you understand better how love is the essence of the divine nature, of your nature and of all creation.

Notes

Day 5: I Am Created by Love in Order to Love

God calls you because God is love and you are part of that love. This is what we considered yesterday and I said it might seem to you somewhat abstract and remote, whereas in actual fact it is something very down to earth with immediately practical consequences.

Because if God is love and we are made to be with God, then we are made by love in order to love. In other words, our whole purpose in life is to learn what love is or, better put, to learn how to love. This is why we are in the world, and if we miss out on this, whatever else we might learn, whatever else we might do or achieve, we have missed out on the most important thing of all. This is what Jesus described to Martha as the 'one thing necessary'.

This has been explained very clearly by Pope John Paul II in a letter to families:

> God created man in his own image and likeness: calling him to existence through love, He called him at the same time for love. God is love and in himself He lives a mystery of personal loving communion. Creating the human race in his own image and continually keeping it in being, God inscribed in the humanity of man and woman the vocation, and thus the capacity and responsibility, of love and communion. Love is therefore the fundamental and innate vocation of every human being. (*Familiaris Consortio* 11)

In another passage he puts it even more strongly:

> Man cannot live without love. He remains a being
> that is incomprehensible for himself, his life is
> senseless, if love is not revealed to him, if he does not
> encounter love, if he does not experience it and make
> it his own, if he does not participate intimately in it.
> (*Redemptor Hominis* 10)

The third Preface in the Mass for Marriage also expresses
this truth in unequivocal terms: 'You created man in love
to share your divine life ... Love is man's origin, love is
his constant calling, love is his fulfilment in heaven'
(*Roman Missal*).

Finally the *Catechism of the Catholic Church* puts it in
these words: 'God who created man out of love also calls
him to love – the fundamental and innate vocation of
every human being. For man is created in the image and
likeness of God who is himself love' (1604).

This statement is repeated in the *Compendium of the
Social Doctrine of the Church*:

> The revelation in Christ of the mystery of God as
> Trinitarian love is at the same time the revelation of
> the vocation of the human person to love ... In the
> communion of love that is God, and in which the
> Three Divine Persons mutually love one another and
> are one God, the human person is called to discover
> the origin and goal of his existence and of history. (34)

I hope you will forgive all these quotations but I believe
they are very important. They show beyond any doubt that
it is no exaggeration to say that to love another is the whole
purpose of our existence, the deepest craving of our being.

And what does this love consist in? It is the same as the love which is the essence of the Trinity: a total giving and receiving of self. And the more we give, the more we will receive, the more we are. This is the great paradox of our being: the struggle between egoism (self-love) and altruism (love of the other). If we die, we find life. If we die to love of self (egoism) we come alive in love of another (altruism).

Teilhard also saw this very clearly. He gives a beautiful and profound definition of love:

> To love is to discover and complete oneself in someone other than oneself, an act impossible of general realization on earth so long as each man can see in his neighbour no more than a closed fragment following its own course through the world. It is precisely this state of isolation that will end if we begin to discover in each other not merely the elements of one and the same thing, but of a single spirit in search of itself. (*The Future of Man*, p. 95)

All of the above can be illustrated, if you will forgive me and can remember your mathematics, in a very simple graph. If you have a pencil and paper handy, try to draw it as I explain. The vertical axis measures the quality of love, starting from pure egoism (point zero) to pure altruism (point 100), in other words, from pure selfishness to pure selflessness. The horizontal axis measures the years of a human life, also starting from point zero and going up to point 100, if you get that far. At birth we all start at point zero. There is nothing more selfish or egoistic than a newly born baby, which is only aware of its own immediate physical needs. If they aren't satisfied, it starts to yell. This is, of course, necessary for its survival, but the whole process of growing up, or 'socialisation' as the psychologists say, is the gradual discovery that there are other people and other needs in the world.

This journey of discovery begins with the infant's own parents and then, a traumatic moment, if and when another child is born in the family and the first child ceases to be the centre of the universe. Another traumatic moment is leaving home to start school for the first time and discovering there are now thirty or more children all competing for the teacher's attention. And as the horizons of life broaden, contact with increasing numbers of people in different circumstances can and should provide a real apprenticeship in the art of true love. But, with one exception, it seems almost inconceivable that anyone, even the greatest of saints such as a Mother Teresa, could arrive at the point of pure altruism which supposes a total gift of self to the other, and therefore the condition for, and possibility of, sharing fully in the life of God who is pure love. The possible exception is the martyr, who makes a complete offering of his or her life to God.

We often talk about life being a journey. Perhaps you can now see more clearly that it is a journey in love and towards love, with the quality of that love changing all the time. For prayer and reflection today, I suggest you look at the quality of love in your own life and ask God to show you if and how it is changing.

Notes

Day 6: From Egoism to Altruism

Yesterday you were contemplating love and perhaps even drawing a graph. It was a graph intended to measure the quality of love in your life. It attempted to show how all of us should be moving away from the purely selfish love with which we were all born towards a completely unselfish love to which we need to attain before we can share fully in God's own love, which is the purpose of our creation.

We are all somewhere on this graph. We can even plot our progress on it. We have to pick our age, now or sometime in the past, and try to determine at that moment what percentage of our love was still egoistic and what percentage altruistic or unselfish. But since no person is a perfect judge in their own case, you or I might not be the best people to do this. We might get a more accurate picture from another person or relative who really knows us well.

However, a uniform progress on the graph would be a straight line 45 degrees from each axis. But this is unlikely since life, with its ups and downs, usually follows a crooked course, sometimes going upwards, sometimes downwards. At the moment of death we remain fixed at a given point. If it is less than 100, then additional purification is needed to eliminate all traces of egoism – hence the doctrine of purgatory. And if, God forbid, we die on level zero, we are incapable of opening up to another since we are totally absorbed in ourselves. This seems to me a fair definition of hell: not being able to love another in the full knowledge that to do so is the whole purpose of our existence. Hopefully none of us will be in this category, which may exist only in theory since Jesus came to save us all. We have to believe in the possibility of hell since Jesus spoke much about it, but we don't have to believe there is anyone in it. In the Mass we pray to God for 'all the dead whose fate is known to you alone' (*Roman Missal*, Canon 4).

Most of us should at least be moving, or be capable of being moved, in the right direction. This is towards the union with God which constitutes the bliss of heaven. It involves a total going out of oneself which is the meaning of the word ecstasy (*ekstasis* in Greek). The joy of heaven is sometimes described as consisting in the 'beatific' or 'ecstatic' vision which, precisely because it consists in a total going out of oneself, we can't visualise or imagine, as Jesus told us. Perhaps the nearest we can get to it is the type of ecstasy we occasionally experience here on earth when the feeling is so strong we become unaware of the passing of time or where we are.

'God is love' is the title of the first encyclical letter written by Benedict XVI shortly after he became Pope. In it he talks about ecstasy as being part of a journey we are all on. He says:

> Love is indeed 'ecstasy', not in the sense of a moment of intoxication, but rather as a journey, an ongoing exodus out of the closed inward-looking self towards its liberation through self-giving, and thus towards authentic self-discovery and indeed the discovery of God. (*Deus Caritas Est* 6)

So far we have been using the one word 'love'. But as you and many realise well, it is a word that means several different things and can be much misused. In the same letter, the Pope distinguishes between what are perhaps the two most important types of love: erotic love or '*eros*', and '*agape*', the word for love used in the New Testament. *Eros* reduced to pure sex, as the Pope points out, 'has become a commodity, a mere "thing" to be bought and sold, or rather, the human person becomes a commodity'. *Eros* is not bad in itself but needs to be disciplined and purified, because 'true *eros* tends to rise "in ecstasy" towards the Divine, to lead us beyond ourselves; yet for this very reason it calls for a path of ascent, renunciation, purification and healing' (*Deus Caritas Est* 5). If this happens, *eros* begins to turn into *agape,* as illustrated on the graph.

A final quote from the Pope's letter serves to confirm this and explain the meaning of *agape*: 'Love becomes concern and care for the other. No longer is it self-seeking, a sinking in the intoxication of happiness; instead it seeks the good of the beloved: it becomes renunciation and it is ready, and even willing, for sacrifice' (*Deus Caritas Est* 6). St Paul clearly recognised that love should be the main force in a person's life. He writes:

> All the commandments: *You shall not commit adultery, you shall not kill, you shall not steal, you shall not covet,* and so on, are summed up in this single command: *You must love your neighbour as yourself.* Love is the one thing that cannot hurt your neighbour; that is why it is the answer to every one of the commandments. (Romans 13:9–10)

And St John adds: 'If we love each other, God lives in us and his love is perfected in us' (1 John 4:12).

All of the above applies equally to love in marriage.

At the outset it usually consists in a strong physical and emotional attraction, which masks a high degree of egoism. It is necessary to bring a couple together, but it does not represent the height of married love as the media or pop operas would sometimes have us believe, since the attraction is bound to diminish over time or even disappear completely. It is therefore necessary to discover a deeper, more mature and altruistic form of love that seeks to give rather than receive. Less glamorous or dramatic, this is what enables a couple to grow ever more closely together over the years in the mutual gift of each to the other. It is, however, a love that calls for sacrifice and even suffering.

I would like to suggest that, in your prayer today, you look at the love in your own life and try to see in which way it is moving. You can look also at the love of Jesus which moved steadily towards an absolute love consisting in the total gift of himself on a cross.

Notes

Day 7: Use of Things: Climate Change

If our purpose in life is to move towards the completely unselfish love we need in order to share in God's life, then we must take a very careful look at the way we use the things God has put at our disposal in our lives and in the world. This is the theme I wish to propose to you today for your reflection and prayer.

The things I am referring to comprise our possessions, our relationships with others including our own family, and also all the resources of the planet. All these can either help us reach our goal or lead us away from it. Therefore our 'use of creatures', to use the traditional term, is a key issue requiring much attention. I need to distinguish carefully between those helping towards my end and those standing in the way of it.

But it should be noted this does not depend so much on the thing or person within itself or him- or herself, but on the use I make of it or them. Jesus explained this point well to the Jews who taught some things were 'impure' in themselves. He said: 'What goes into the mouth does not make a man unclean; it is what comes out of the mouth that makes him unclean' (Matthew 15:10–11). And he explains this:

'Things that come out of the mouth come from the heart, and it is these that make a man unclean. For from the heart come evil intentions: adultery, fornication, theft, perjury, slander. These are the things that make a man unclean.' (Matthew 15: 18–20)

This would seem a good place to reflect on the destruction of the world through global warming, which is becoming an increasingly serious threat to humanity and is very much concerned with our use or misuse of creation.

As you well know, this has become a major issue for discussion and there are differing views on it. But what now seems clear beyond any doubt, and agreed by the majority of scientists even though some may differ over details, is that, for the first time in history, mankind can and is destroying the world and making it uninhabitable for future generations.

If nothing is done to counter this, it will start happening very soon, certainly in the lifetime of our own children. Recent freak weather in many parts of the world would seem to indicate it is beginning to happen already.

The scientists claim (see for example the authoritative Stern Report on the *Economics of Climate Change* or the recent and even more authoritative UN *Report of the Intergovernmental Panel on Climate Change*) that even a modest rise in temperature of between two to three degrees over the next fifty years would lead to:

– massive flood risks from melting glaciers;
– rising sea levels making over 200 million people permanently displaced;
– a dramatic fall in crop yields and food production of up to 50 per cent in some areas;
– 40 per cent of all plant and animal species becoming extinct;
– a marked increase in hurricanes, deluges, droughts and heat waves.

If nothing is done to correct it, at our present rate the rise in temperature will be much higher, and therefore the results more serious and unavoidable. The amount of carbon dioxide in the atmosphere has already reached its highest level in human history and is nudging ever closer to what is described as a point of no return. The experts agree there is still time for action but it is running out fast.

Though the richer nations have contributed and continue to contribute most to greenhouse gas emissions, the experts argue that the effects will fall mainly on the poor countries and peoples least able to take action against them. So the issue of justice also enters.

This is not meant to be a socio-economic treatise and you must excuse me for the above, which you may already be very familiar with. But, and this is partly my justification, churches and others emphasise that this is not a purely economic or social problem, but a matter of morality and ethics. We are therefore all involved from the mere fact of being human beings, and more so if we are Christians.

Pope John Paul II called for an 'ecological conversion'. We have to realise we are meant to be 'stewards of creation' and that the world has been given us to use and develop in accordance with God's plan. We have no right to destroy it either now or for future generations.

This is well expressed – my last quotation, you will be happy to learn – in the *Catechism of the Catholic Church*, and provides a good yardstick for self-examination that I encourage you to use.

> The seventh commandment enjoins respect for the integrity of creation. Animals, like plants and inanimate beings, are by nature destined for the

common good of past, present and future humanity. Use of the mineral, vegetable and animal resources of the universe cannot be divorced from respect for moral imperatives. Man's dominion over inanimate and other living beings granted by the Creator is not absolute; it is limited by concern for the quality of life of his neighbour, including generations to come; it requires a religious respect for the integrity of creation. (2415)

Your prayer today should be practical and down to earth. What can or should you be doing, as a Christian or someone concerned with issues of good and evil, to remedy the situation described above?

Notes

Day 8: The Sin of the World

Most retreats are based, to a greater or lesser extent, on the Spiritual Exercises of St Ignatius, who was officially declared patron of spiritual exercises and retreats by Pope Pius XI. His Exercises were notes for prayer and reflection based on his own conversion experience when still a layman. I therefore expect to be quoting him quite a lot in the days to come, since the thoughts I am sharing with you are based closely on his Exercises. The official title he gave them was: 'Spiritual Exercises having as their purpose the overcoming of self and the ordering of one's life on the basis of a decision made in freedom from any ill-ordered attachments'. This is a bit of a mouthful, but it means they are an attempt to re-order our lives, with God's help, and get rid of anything that prevents us from moving closer to the selfless love that we have seen is the whole purpose of our existence.

The things in our lives, ranging from ideas, personal relations or physical things we can touch and see, are all there to be used by us only in so far as they help us achieve our purpose in life. Unfortunately we can also misuse them and they become obstacles rather than helps. We do this, as Ignatius points out, because of disordered inclinations or attachments moving us in the wrong direction. This applies to all those habits and actions or lack of actions that increase our egoism or selfish love, and are normally called sins. So a consideration of sin, both in the world and our own personal lives, is an essential part of making a retreat.

It doesn't require much investigation to conclude that the world as a whole has rejected God's call to discover what true love is and build a civilisation based on it. The signs of this rejection and its consequences are only too evident and well known to us all. One cannot turn on the radio or watch TV without being overwhelmed by disaster stories from all over the world. Darfur, Gaza, the Middle East, Burma, Afghanistan, Iraq, Zimbabwe are just a few of the names that immediately spring to mind at the present time.

And so often these situations of violence are structural. That is, they depend on unjust social structures imposed and maintained by small groups of the wealthy and powerful, both within countries and between them.

The United Nations Development Programme in its annual report is continually pointing out that never has there been so much wealth in the world and never has it been so unequally divided. *Forbes Magazine*, which every year measures the wealth of the wealthiest, claims for the first time that the 400 richest Americans are no longer millionaires, but billionaires. It has been calculated that the three wealthiest people in the world have assets that exceed the total wealth of the 48 least developed countries with a combined population of hundreds of millions.

On the other side of the picture, as a recent book puts it:

Almost three billion people live on less than two dollars a day. Eight hundred and forty million people in the world don't have enough to eat. Ten million children die every year from easily preventable diseases. AIDS is killing three million people a year and is still spreading. One billion people in the world

> lack access to clean water; two billion lack access to
> sanitation. One billion adults are illiterate. About a
> quarter of the children in the poor countries do not
> finish primary school. (William Easterly, *The White
> Man's Burden*, OUP 2006, p. 7)

And so on and so on. One could go on quoting figures
such as these all day. I end with one final one from the
United Nations Development Programme Report of
1998:

> People in Europe and North America now spend $37
> billion on pet food, perfumes and cosmetics. This
> figure would provide basic education, water and
> sanitation, basic health and nutrition for all those now
> deprived of it and still leave $9 billion over.

This situation has been described by the head of FAO as
a 'shameful fact', a 'terrible indictment of the world in
2007', 'an issue that needs to be solved immediately'.
Forty years ago in his great letter on *The Development of
Peoples*, Pope Paul VI described the 'scandal of
development' as an 'outrage against humanity'. And Pope
John Paul II spoke of the pervading 'structures of sin',
particularly characterised by 'the all- consuming desire
for profit and the thirst for power' in all cultures in *On
Social Concern* 37). This is certainly not the sort of world
intended by God. As the Antilles Bishops put it: 'Any
society in which a few control most of the wealth and
the masses are left in want is a sinful society' (*Justice &
Peace in a New Caribbean* §34).

But perhaps the worst of all is that this grotesque
situation is getting worse all the time. Owing to unjust
structures, especially in the areas of trade and debt, the

so-called aid of the wealthy countries to the poor is actually flowing in the opposite direction. The massive net transfer of wealth and resources from the poorer countries to the wealthy is intolerable and surely constitutes the single greatest scandal of our age. It is as though the wealthy nations are continuing, just as they did in the colonial times of the past, to live off the backs of the poor and exploit them with impunity.

I am sure you already know all this and hope you will excuse my outburst of statistics. The frustrating thing is that the experts know exactly what needs to be done to set things right, but the political will is lacking to take the necessary action. For me this is an outstanding example of the effects of sin in the world. I suggest you spend your prayer time today reflecting on this and looking at some of the examples you yourself know or have experienced.

Notes

Day 9: My Sin

I wonder what your reaction was to yesterday's consideration of the evil and injustice in the world? I ask this because it affects different people in different ways.

Some say: 'What has all this got to do with me? I am not responsible. I have my job to do, my own life to lead. I should get on with these, and leave the world's problems to those more capable of dealing with them'. Others say: 'Even if I may be partly responsible, I am only one person and the problems are so complex and vast that I can't possibly have any effect on them, even if I understood them properly which I don't. I feel powerless and inadequate.'

Yet you and I are integral parts of the sinful structures we looked at yesterday. This is the first thing we have to realise and the theme I would like to suggest for your prayer today.

If sin is a rejection of love, an egoistic turning in on self, a denial of God's plan both for me and the universe, then my sin adds to the evil in the world and I cannot separate myself from it. My sin and your sin increase the general sinfulness in the world and make it a worse place. They lower the amount of true love in the universe and thus help to destroy attempts to form a civilisation built on love. In a hymn for the morning prayer of the Church on Tuesdays we pray: 'The love that we have wasted, O God of love, renew'. Our sin is precisely a wastage of love.

So it is extremely important to consider carefully the dimension of sin in my present life. How am I an obstacle to the creative and loving action of God in the world? How am I blocking the work God wants to carry out through me, and thus lessening the value of my own work and even making it counter-productive? These are the questions you can ask yourself during today's prayer.

It is not easy to understand or even admit one's own sinfulness and we can so easily fool ourselves. One way of doing this is by remaining on the surface of things and concentrating only on trivial misdemeanours. We have to try to examine the roots of our sinfulness. There are areas of my life of which I am probably unaware or don't want to face up to. Rather than concentrate on specific and often superficial sins, we should try to go beneath the surface in an attempt to understand what causes them. This can mean examining our tendencies, urges, the hidden drives that often determine our actions.

Note that it is not a question of making an examination of conscience as we might do before going to confession. As already said, this carries the risk of limiting ourselves to superficial and less important things. It is a question of uncovering the blind spots in my life, things that I don't want to admit even to myself.

One of the paradoxes in all this is that we cannot appreciate our sinfulness in any depth without coming nearer to God. It is striking how, in the lives of so many saints, the holier they become, the more they seem to realise they are sinners and the greater their sin seems to them. One of the early desert fathers wrote: 'The nearer a person approaches to God, the greater sinner they see themselves to be.'

You may remember how the ancient Greeks put self-knowledge as the basis of all wisdom. You and I want to beg God today for this true knowledge of ourselves in the deepest and most hidden parts of our being.

We will then begin to have an interior knowledge of our sins and an abhorrence for them. And this should lead us to a sense of personal shame and a determination to put our lives in order.

Suggestions for today's prayer have already been made above. If you find it helpful, you could also consider any of the penitents in the New Testament.

- Zacchaeus (Luke 19:1–10).
- The woman who was a sinner (Luke 7:36–50).
- The adulterous woman (John 8:1–11).
- The good thief (Luke 23:39–43).
- The prodigal son (Luke 15:11–31).

Notes

Day 10: God's Forgiveness

We have looked at sin in the world with its dreadful consequences and my personal part in this, yours and mine. How should we respond? Is there any hope or is all gloom and despair?

Well, we can't answer this question until we consider how God responds. And here the answer is clear and unequivocal.

God forgives immediately and completely without harbouring any grudges or imposing any punishments. As Isaiah puts it, 'you have thrust all my sins behind your back' (Isaiah 38:17). God's attitude is summed up beautifully in the behaviour of the father in the parable of the prodigal son. Even though the father would have been perfectly justified in imposing some sort of penalty on the son, and even though the son seems to have repented mainly because he was hungry and unhappy in the country where he had gone, the father pays no attention to any of this but not only gives his son an immediate and complete pardon but welcomes him with great joy and happiness.

For, as Jesus himself said, 'There will be more rejoicing in heaven over one repentant sinner than over ninety-nine virtuous men who have no need of repentance' (Luke 15:7). And the whole of his life is full of notable examples of how readily and completely he forgave sins – the good thief, Mary Magdalene, Zacchaeus, and so many others.

In the Bible God says:

What! Am I likely to take pleasure in the death of a
wicked man – it is the Lord Yahweh who speaks –
and not prefer to see him renounce his wickedness
and live? . . . I take no pleasure in the death of anyone
– it is the Lord Yahweh who speaks. Repent and live!
(Ezekiel 18:23 and 32)

And one of the most beautiful of the psalms describes
God as being 'always merciful and tender-hearted, slow
to anger, always loving, always loyal' (Psalm 86:15).
Imagine Jesus saying to you the words the prophet Joel
puts in God's mouth:

'Come back to me with all your heart . . .'
Let your hearts be broken, not your garments torn,
turn to Yahweh your God again,
for he is all tenderness and compassion,
slow to anger, rich in graciousness,
and ready to relent. (Joel 2:12–13)

How then should I, you and I, react to this loving
kindness of God?

The first thing is to accept it in wonder and humility.
One commentator on the Exercises has said that our
attitude must be 'to stand without defences before the
gratuity of God's love'. 'Without defences' means not
putting up any barriers or hiding behind excuses, but
being ready to follow whatever path God indicates. At
the same time we should feel a sense of shame and a
determination to avoid sin in the future.

This will call for a conversion. Not a conversion in
the sense of finding a new faith, but in acknowledging
that there is something which needs changing in my life.
This applies to all of us, to you as well as me, because no

one can claim if honest that there is nothing that needs to be changed in his or her life.

A retreat is precisely to help us find out what it is that needs to be changed and to give us the strength and courage to take the practical steps required to change it. This can certainly cost us but it is an accurate measure of our love for God in return for God's love of us. As another commentator on the Exercises has put it, our desire for conversion 'arises out of the literally heart-breaking experience of being loved and forgiven'.

And we can only fully experience this, not in our minds or understanding, but in our hearts and our feelings. Hence it is important to seek this grace from God. Another beautiful passage in the Bible has God saying this to his chosen people:

> I am going to take you from among the nations and gather you together from all the foreign countries, and bring you home to your own land. I shall pour clean water over you and you will be cleansed; I shall cleanse you of all your defilement and all your idols. I shall give you a new heart, and put a new spirit in you; I shall remove the heart of stone from your bodies and give you a heart of flesh instead. I shall put my spirit in you, and make you keep my laws and sincerely respect my observances. You will live in the land which I gave your ancestors. You shall be my people and I will be your God. (Ezekiel 36:24–28)

This is how God will help us too towards the conversion we are looking for. Pray today for this personal conversion of the heart, for this heart of flesh that God offers. And we must not forget that true conversion should also include a greater concern for the sins of the world. As Archbishop

Romero of El Salvador said – and this is my final quotation:

> A true Christian conversion in today's world must unmask the social mechanisms which turn the worker or rural peasant into marginal people. Why is there only pay for the rural peasant at the time of the coffee or cotton crops or the sugar harvest? Why does this society need to have peasants without work, badly paid workers, people without a fair wage? These mechanisms must be uncovered, not as if we were students of sociology or economics, but as Christians, so as not to be accomplices of a system that is making people ever poorer, more marginalised, in greater need. (16 December 1979)

In your prayer today, reflect on the way God forgives you and therefore how you too should respond.

Notes

Day 11: The Good Leader

St Ignatius divided his Spiritual Exercises into four weeks of unequal length, of which the first two are usually the most important. The purpose of the first week is to take a close look at my life to try and see in which way it is moving, that is, towards or away from its ultimate goal. This will include a consideration of sin and evil since these are the things that impel it to travel in the wrong direction, away from its ultimate goal.

This is precisely what we have been doing in the retreat up till now. Hopefully you will now have a clearer picture of where you are going, of where you ought to be going, and the beginning of an idea of how you might get there.

The second week, which we start today, is in many ways the key or decisive one. Its purpose is to help you take the necessary steps or decisions to correct the wrong directions in your life and put you back on the right path. For some people this will require a major decision about the future of their lives. It was precisely for them that Ignatius composed and usually gave his Spiritual Exercises. The classic example is his friend Francis Xavier, all set on earthly wealth and glory, until Ignatius finally got through to him with the message: 'What does it profit a man to gain the whole world but suffer the loss of his own soul?'

But for most people the major choices in their lives will have already been made, and the Exercises serve more to identify a change or adaptation of something not working well in their present situation. And no one can say with honesty there is nothing that needs changing in my life. For such people it will not be necessary to follow the full election process Ignatius sets out.

You will know to which category you belong. But for all of us, the call is to follow the direction the Lord indicates and to do so with as much generosity as we can.

At the beginning of the retreat you reflected on the fact that God was calling you by name, just as Abraham or Samuel were called. But it was a general call, not to any specific mission, but to be ready and disposed for anything.

Now, after contemplating the effects of sin in the world and also your own part in it, you should have a clearer idea of what his call is and how urgent it is. It is the call of Christ to share in his mission to combat sin and thus bring salvation to the whole world and to ourselves. What we have to consider now is how we can best share in this mission in whatever situation we find ourselves. And our prayer today is that we may not be deaf to God's call but ready to accept it with alacrity and give it the best we possibly can.

To help us do this, Ignatius suggests we look at leadership or someone we really admire and would like to follow. Think of any good or inspiring leader you may know or have read about. Two that spring immediately to my mind are Mahatma Gandhi and Nelson Mandela, but these may seem somewhat awesome and distant figures. I am sure you can come up with others.

Reflect now for a few moments on what the qualities are that make them good leaders or role models. There are probably a whole range of them including a variety of skills the modern leader needs today. But I feel sure that underlying them all is the fact that they are not out for themselves but are utterly dedicated to the service of others. What counts for them is not their own power or prestige but the cause they are pursuing in the interests of others and for which they are prepared to accept sacrifices and even suffering. It is precisely this that attracts others to follow them since they know they will not be required to do anything the leader hasn't already done before them. They also know it will help them for, as Gandhi put it well: 'The best way to find yourself is to lose yourself in the service of others.'

But whoever you choose as leader, however dedicated he or she may be, there is one who outshines any leader we can imagine. St John relates in his gospel how, on the last night he was able to spend with his apostles, while they were already seated at table to have supper, Jesus

> got up from table, removed his outer garment and, taking a towel, wrapped it round his waist; he then poured water into a basin and began to wash the disciples' feet and to wipe them with the towel he was wearing. (John 13:4–5)

The disciples were astounded and Jesus had to explain to them what he was doing:

> 'You call me Master and Lord, and rightly; so I am. If I, then, the Lord and Master, have washed your feet, you should wash each other's feet. I have given you an example so that you may copy what I have done to you.' (John 13:13–15)

This is the true leadership Jesus exercised throughout his life, emphasising that he came 'not to be served but to serve, and to give his life as a ransom for many' (Matthew 20:25–28).

This is the leader who is now inviting you to join him and to share his mission with him, even though some pain or suffering may be involved.

In your prayer today, reflect on the qualities of true leadership, and on the call or invitation Jesus is making to you. And make your act of offering to him, that you want to follow him to the very best of your ability and put at his disposal all the gifts and skills you have.

Notes

Day 12: The Annunciation

Before looking at the sort of criteria which should determine your response to follow God's call more closely, it is worth looking at the criteria which determined the choice of Jesus to become man in order to save us. We can see these criteria most clearly in the two great events at the beginning of his life: the Incarnation and the Nativity. I propose you spend today looking at and praying about the Incarnation.

There several ways of doing this. St Ignatius suggests a contemplation in which we imagine we are actually present at the scene, watching what the people are doing and hearing what they are saying to each other.

This may not suit everyone. So Ignatius also offers some thoughts or points to consider.

But the first thing is to remind ourselves of the incident we are going to look at. In this case it is the visit of the Angel Gabriel to Mary in which he announces God's plan to her. To put it mildly, she is surprised and afraid but, with more explanations from the Angel, finally accepts with a wonderful act of faith and obedience: 'I am the handmaid of the Lord: let what you have said be done to me' (see Luke 1:26–38).

Then, very important, we are to ask God what we want to obtain. This is how Ignatius puts it: 'To ask for inner knowledge of the Lord who became human for me so that I might better love and follow him'. A popular version of this request is attributed to St Richard of Chichester: 'Lord, may I know you more clearly, love you more dearly, and follow you more nearly.'

The first point Ignatius suggests is to look at the different persons involved. There are all the people on the face of the earth, 'in all their diversity of dress and appearance, some white and some black, some in peace and others at war, some weeping and others laughing, some healthy, others sick, some being born and others dying, etc.' Today we might add: some rich, others poor, some learned and powerful, others ignorant and weak, some in the centre of things, others on the margin of society. We then consider the three persons of the Holy Trinity, looking at the world from the vantage point they have and seeing so many millions searching and longing for the truth, like sheep without a shepherd, as Jesus put it. Finally we see Our Lady and the Angel who greets her.

Second, we imagine what they are saying to each other. In the case of Mary and the Angel we already know. With regard to the people on the earth, the possibilities are almost infinite but we should not forget whose voices are heard, those who control the communications media, who are taken in by them. Nor should we forget the vast numbers who are voiceless or the many places where those who speak are not allowed to say what they really think. To imagine the three Divine Persons speaking among themselves is to put God in time as well as space. We cannot understand how, in eternity, a decision was reached to redeem the human race through Jesus Christ becoming a man. But this is what happened.

Lastly we consider what the different persons are doing. Here again with Mary and the Angel we already know. Mary accepts the proposal and the Angel's mission is a success. And with the people on the earth, the possibilities are again almost infinite. But, as already mentioned earlier on, the thing that would perhaps most astonish an onlooker from outer space is the totally unbalanced distribution of wealth and resources that has a small minority living in abundant luxury while the vast majority have to scrape a living in order to survive. With regard to God's activity – the incarnation takes place.

At the end of all this, Ignatius adds one of his favourite phrases: 'Then I will reflect to draw profit from each of these things.' Your own reflection could be nourished by a whole variety of considerations or questions. Here are a few:

1. Why was a simple, illiterate village girl from an insignificant colonial country chosen to be mother of God?
2. Why did the Incarnation, which has to be considered the central event of human history, depend on Mary's acceptance?
3. From the moment of Mary's 'yes', 'the power of the Most High covered her with its shadow', and she became pregnant through the Holy Spirit. One wonders to what extent she realised this from the very start.
4. What does this extraordinary scene have to say to me about my life?

Your prayer should end with what Ignatius calls a 'colloquy'. This is a conversation 'according to my inner feelings' with 'the three Divine Persons, or . . . the eternal Word who has become human for me, or . . . his mother, Our Lady'. In it you should ask that you may the better follow and imitate Our Lord, thus newly incarnate.

Notes

Day 13: The Nativity

Following St Ignatius, I suggest you spend your prayer time today contemplating and reflecting on Our Lord's nativity. The purpose is the same as yesterday's. That is, 'to' look at the criteria which determined Jesus' coming into the world so as to have a better idea of the criteria which should determine your response to his call.

The Christmas scene is so well known to us that it is difficult to say anything about it that is new or that we don't already know. In some ways this is a disadvantage since, as the saying goes, familiarity breeds contempt. Most of us have long since lost the wonder and surprise it should inspire.

However it is worth making an effort not only to see the well-known events, but also to ask ourselves why. What message is Christ trying to send us by being born in a cave or stable, because there was no room at the inn? What a humiliation this must have been for Mary and Joseph who, like parents everywhere, had probably been carefully preparing for his birth. Why should this have been wished on them? And why, on this momentous event in human history, are the only people who knew about it a handful of simple, uneducated shepherds who happened to be watching their flocks nearby?

One of the answers to these three questions is contained in the word 'poverty'. Jesus chose to be born in poverty and seeming abandonment to teach us that God does not need human means and resources to do his work.

But Jesus does need us. And this is his call: to join him in his work of bringing love and salvation to the world. But to do this, we have to rely not on ourselves, not on wealth, influence, possessions, or any skills we may have, but on God working through us. The more we allow this, the more we do it in his way, the more effective we will be.

This was a lesson Jesus repeated many times in his life. When he sent out the twelve on their first mission, he told them: 'Take nothing for the journey: neither staff, nor haversack, nor bread, nor money; and let none of you take a spare tunic' (Luke 9:3–4). They would have to rely entirely on God and it was this that gave strength to their words, as they reported to Jesus on their return. At the feeding of the five thousand, Jesus told the apostles to feed the people themselves. When they replied: 'All we have with us is five loaves and two fish', he invited the people to sit down and 'they all ate as much as they wanted' (Matthew 15:16–21). Not long after, when the apostles had crossed the lake but forgotten to take any food with them, Jesus chided them saying:

> 'Men of little faith, why are you talking among yourselves about having no bread? Do you not yet understand? Do you not remember the five loaves for the five thousand and the number of baskets you collected? Or the seven loaves for the four thousand and the number of baskets you collected?' (Matthew 16:8–10)

The lesson should at least be clear to us, to you and me. If we let Jesus work though us by putting ourselves completely in his hands, we too can achieve wonders. The lives of so many saints have shown this. We can almost say the weaker and more helpless they were, the more God's power shone through them. If we rely on ourselves, we are limited to five loaves and two fishes which don't go very far. If we rely on God, we become like the branch on the vine: 'Whoever remains in me, with me in him, bears fruit in plenty' (John 15:5).

In choosing to be born poor, Jesus was not trying to glorify poverty for its own sake. Still less was he ratifying the conditions of so many poor people in the world, either in his time or in ours. The Bible condemns and rejects poverty as a scandal. God gave the earth and all it contains to everyone. Freedom from poverty is one of the signs of his Kingdom where the hungry are blessed because they will have their fill.

The fundamental reason why Jesus chose to be born poor, live among the poor and die owning nothing, is that love the theologians call 'kenosis', the emptying out of oneself. St Paul describes it well:

> His state was divine,
> yet he did not cling
> to his equality with God
> but emptied himself
> to assume the condition of a slave,
> and become as men are;
> and being as all men are,
> he was humbler yet,
> even to accepting death,
> death on a cross.

And it was because of this that 'God raised him high' (Philippians 2:6–9).

I hope you will forgive all these quotations and at least find some of them useful for your prayer. I want to end with one last one, also from St Paul, since I think it sums up and explains admirably why Jesus chose to be born poor. 'Remember how generous the Lord Jesus was: he was rich, but he became poor for your sake, to make you rich out of his poverty' (2 Corinthians 8:9). Let us consider how we are rich out of his poverty.

Notes

Day 14: Two Standards

St Ignatius' meditation under the title 'On Two Standards' already introduces the beginning of the process of choice, or the 'Election', which is the whole purpose of the retreat. It promotes the dispositions we need in order to be able to hear Christ's call. It prepares the retreatant for a particular election, either of a state of life or for some change in his or her present life, by looking at the values Christ adopted in his life, which are so different from those normally adopted by the world around us.

The core of the meditation is a comparison between the tactics and strategies of the Evil One and the tactics and strategies of Christ. It is based on the experience Jesus underwent in the desert where the Spirit led him immediately after his baptism and before the beginning of his public life.

The three evangelists known as the 'synoptics' all give an account of this (Matthew 4:1–11; Mark 1:12–13; Luke 4:1–13) so there is a choice of texts for today's prayer. I shall mainly rely on Matthew's version, which is perhaps the fullest and clearest, but with occasional references to Luke.

As usual, Ignatius instructs us to ask for what we want. Here

> it will be to ask for knowledge of the deceptions practised by the evil leader and for help to guard against them, and also for knowledge of the true life revealed by the supreme and true Commander, and for grace to imitate him.

He then imagines Lucifer instructing his demons to lay traps for people and bind them with chains, a bit like Screwtape in C. S. Lewis's *Screwtape Letters*.

> They are to tempt them first to crave after riches (the enemy's usual tactic), so that they might come more readily to the empty honours of the world, and in the end to unbounded pride. Therefore the first step is riches, the second, honour, and the third, pride; from these three steps the enemy leads people on to every other vice.

This is a masterful analysis that shows Ignatius, reflecting on his own experience, as a psychiatrist whose diagnosis is just as relevant today. As St Paul puts it to Timothy: 'The love of money is the root of all evils' (1 Timothy 6:10).

The tempter in the desert was equally skilled. After forty days there without eating, Jesus was hungry. So the devil said to him: 'If you are the Son of God, tell these stones to turn into a loaves'. But Jesus replied: 'Scripture says: *Man does not live on bread alone, but on every word that comes from the mouth of God.*' Riches in themselves are no solution, especially when obtained through false or unjust practices. Our world of today knows this only too well.

The second temptation concerns honour or power.

> The devil then took him to the holy city and made him stand on the parapet of the Temple. 'If you are the Son of God', he said 'throw yourself down; for scripture says: *He will put you in his angels' charge, and they will support you in their hands in case you hurt your foot against a stone*'. Jesus said to him, 'Scripture also says: *You must not put the Lord your God to the test.*'

Finally, the devil took him to a very high mountain, and

> showed him all the kingdoms of the world and their splendour. 'I will give you all these', he said, 'if you fall at my feet and worship me.' Then Jesus replied, 'Be off, Satan! For Scripture says: *You must worship the Lord your God, and serve him alone.*'

As Father Arrupe emphasised in a talk to former Jesuit students:

> These three temptations express succinctly the three great false hopes of mankind. They are as powerful and compelling as ever in our world of today. Nor is the Church free of them, nor any one of us here present at the moment. It is essential, therefore, we make an effort to understand them and see what effect they have on our personal lives, our families and the society we live in. (*Justice with Faith Today*, p. 230)

Set against these are the three steps or strategies adopted by Christ:

> Therefore there are three steps, first, poverty as opposed to riches, second, humiliation or contempt as opposed to worldly honour, and thirdly humility as opposed to pride. From these three steps they can lead everyone to all the other virtues.

When Jesus said 'My ways are not your ways', he was certainly not exaggerating! As someone once summed it up, our love of power has to be replaced by God's power of love.

The conclusion St Ignatius draws from all this is a very practical one you might find some difficulty in accepting. In the final prayer, he instructs us to ask to be received under God's standard,

> first in the highest spiritual poverty and also, if his Divine Majesty requires this and should be pleased to choose and receive me for it, no less in actual poverty; second in suffering humiliations and insults so as to imitate him more closely, only if I can suffer these without sin on the part of any other person and without displeasure to his Divine Majesty.

This is not an easy prayer to make but we should note carefully that both requests are conditioned by God's will and perhaps leave to God the extent to which they become real in my life. The grace of the Two Standards, as an authoritative commentator has pointed out, is 'that of conversion to an outlook in which humiliation is positively valued, against an outlook in which the basic value is "honour"' (Michael Ivens, *Understanding the Spiritual Exercises*, p. 113). It is a good preparation for the election that follows.

Notes

Day 15: Three Classes of Persons

The next meditation proposed by St Ignatius is on Three Classes of Persons, 'so that we may embrace whatever is the better'. The emphasis is still on the choice that lies ahead of the retreatant in reply to Christ's call, on the demands of the concrete commitment he or she will be making.

In accordance with this, the petition in our prayer should be: 'the grace to choose what is more for the glory of his Divine Majesty and for the salvation of my soul'.

Ignatius asks us to imagine three persons, each of whom has acquired a large fortune (10,000 ducats) 'but not purely, and as would have been right for the love of God'. In other words, some corruption or fast dealing is probably involved. However they all want to be saved and 'to meet God Our Lord in peace'. This means for each getting rid of 'the burden or obstacle arising from the attachment they feel to the thing they have acquired'. But each sets about this in a different way.

'The persons of the *first class* would like to be free of the attachment they have to the acquired possession . . . but they take no means to bring this about until the hour of their death.' In other words, enormous good will and right intentions, but continued procrastination and therefore no action at all until it is too late.

An obvious gospel example of this is the story of the ten bridesmaids, sometimes called the 'wise' and the 'foolish' virgins. They all wanted to accompany the bridegroom with their lamps but he came very late. The wise virgins were able to light theirs because they had taken the precaution of bringing extra oil. The foolish virgins couldn't because they had run out of oil. They went out to buy some, but arrived late and found the door closed. 'Lord, Lord,' they said, 'open the door for us.' But he replied, 'I tell you solemnly, I do not know you' (Matthew 25:11–13).

This would be like the sower's seed that fell 'on rocky ground where it found little soil and sprang up straight away, because there was no depth of earth; and when the sun came up it was scorched and, not having any roots, it withered away' (Mark 4:4–5). As Jesus explained later:

> 'Those who receive the seed on patches of rock are people who, when first they hear the word, welcome it at once with joy. But they have no root in them, they do not last; should some trial come, or some persecution on account of the word, they fall away at once.' (Matthew 4:16–17)

Those of the *second class* want to be free of their attachment, but they want this to be in such a way that they will still retain possession of what they have; so God is to approve of what they themselves want, and there is no decision to relinquish it even if it might be better for them if they did.

This is equivalent to wanting to have one's cake and eat it. The obvious gospel example is the rich young man who wants to follow Jesus but hold on to his wealth. Jesus said to him:

> 'There is one thing you lack. Go and sell everything you own and give the money to the poor, and you will have treasure in heaven; then come, follow me'.

But his face fell at these words and he went away sad, for he was a man of great wealth. (Mark 10:21–22)

It was Jesus himself who said clearly,

'No one can be the slave of two masters: he will either hate the first and love the second, or treat the first with respect and the second with scorn. You cannot be the slave both of God and of money.' (Matthew 6:24)

This is the seed that fell among thorns which grew up and choked it. As Jesus explains, 'The one who received the seed in thorns is the man who hears the word, but the worries of this world and the lure of riches choke the word and so he produces nothing' (Matthew 13:22).

Finally,

Those of the *third class* want to be rid of their attachment; moreover they want to be rid of it in such a way that they also have no inclination to retain their acquisition or not to retain it, but all they want is simply that their wanting or not wanting it should be in accordance with whatever God Our Lord inclines them to want, and as might appear to be more for the service and praise of His Divine Majesty.

Scripture has many examples of these, starting with Abraham, who accepted God's order to sacrifice his own dearly loved son Isaac. After God intervened and provided a solution, Abraham was promised: 'because you have done this, because you have not refused me your son, your only son, I will shower blessings on you, I will make your descendents as many as the stars of heaven and the grains of sand on the seashore' (Genesis 22:1–18).

Examples in the New Testament start with Mary herself, many of the apostles who 'left all to follow Christ', and St Paul, who never looked back after his conversion. This is the seed which fell in good ground and represents those who 'hear the word and accept it and yield a harvest, thirty and sixty and a hundredfold' (Mark 4:20).

The final prayer is to consider which of the three classes you belong to and to ask God for the grace to put you into the third. This will call for the true 'indifference' Ignatius mentions at the outset of the Exercises. It includes not only deciding on what needs to be done to bring your life into line with God's call, but in taking the necessary steps to achieve this, however painful they may turn out to be.

Notes

Day 16: Three Kinds of Humility

The Three Kinds or Degrees of Humility is a short consideration St Ignatius places immediately before the retreatant embarks on the election or decisions needed for a change of life. He does not give it the status of a meditation, but obviously considers it important for the very position it occupies. It is as though he was saying: 'This is the last thing I want you to think about and keep in mind as you start making your resolutions. Therefore I suggest you spend today's prayer and reflection on this simple but profound statement.'

But what does Ignatius mean by 'humility'? As many have pointed out, the word can be misleading, and even off-putting. We already saw something of it in the meditation on the Two Standards. Our Lord's call to his followers was to embrace spiritual, or even actual, poverty since this brings humiliation and contempt. And then he adds: 'from these two things follows humility'. But it is humility in the sense of subjugation to God's law through love.

A recognised expert on the Exercises says:

There is nothing self-denigratory or servile about conceiving one's relationship with God in this way. Humility is in fact nothing other than the love of God, but to call this love 'humility' is to pinpoint especially the quality of other-directedness in love, love as a handing oneself over in trust, letting God be the Lord of one's being. A retreatant who made the Exercises under Ignatius in 1538 describes the modes of humility as 'kinds and degrees of the love of God, and of desiring to obey, imitate and serve his Divine Majesty'. (Ivens, *Understanding the Spiritual Exercises*, p. 123)

Humility, thus understood, is a condition for making a good election or choice. There are, as we shall see, three kinds or degrees. For admission to the election, the first kind of humility is insufficient. The second is both required and sufficient. The third is highly desirable, but not strictly necessary.

The *first degree* consists in this:

That as far as in me lies, I so subject and humble myself that I obey the law of God Our Lord in everything; so much so that even if I were made lord of all created things in this world, or even if my own life on this earth were at stake, I would not make a decision to set about breaking any law, whether divine or human, which obliges me under pain of mortal sin.

Even though the 'minimum', and insufficient for making an election, this could call for heroic courage. We have in recent times been given an outstanding example in the beatification of Franz Jägerstätter, an Austrian farmer and father of three children, who was beheaded by the Nazis in 1943 for refusing to bear arms in Hitler's army. He believed this would have been seriously wrong and, though many friends tried to dissuade him, chose to die rather than give in.

The *second kind of humility* is more perfect than the first. It is present if I find myself at a point where I neither desire nor prefer to be rich rather than poor, to seek fame rather than disgrace, to desire a long rather than a short life, provided it is all the same for the service of God and the good of my soul. Together with this I would not make a decision to set about committing a venial sin, even for the whole of creation or under threat to my own life.

This refers back to the word 'indifference' Ignatius uses at the beginning of the retreat when considering the use of creatures and also in the meditation on the Three Classes of Persons. It does not mean a lack of interest or apathy, but a positive desire for God's will to take priority over any other choice. This is a necessary condition for making a good election.

The *third kind of humility* is the most perfect humility. It is present when my disposition is as follows. Given that the first and second kinds of humility are included, and supposing equal praise and glory of the Divine Majesty, then, in order to imitate Christ Our Lord and to be actually more like him, I want and choose poverty with Christ poor rather than wealth, and humiliations with Christ humiliated rather than fame, and I desire more to be thought worthless and a fool for Christ, who first was taken to be such, rather than to be esteemed as wise and prudent in this world.

This calls for a high degree of sanctity, which you and I may well feel is far out of our reach. Yet Our Lord spoke of this in the Beatitudes, saying 'Happy are you when people abuse you and speak all kinds of calumny against you on my account' (Matthew 5:11) and warned his apostles at the last supper they would suffer much persecution and rejection for his sake (John 15:18 and 16:1–4). They took the lesson to heart since, in the Acts of the Apostles, there are numerous examples of how they suffered for Christ and were happy to do so. St Paul lists all the maltreatments he suffered in announcing the Good News and claims this enabled God's strength to shine through him.

St Ignatius required candidates for the Society to be confronted with this possibility: they should

> desire to clothe themselves with the same garb and uniform of their Lord because of the love and reverence owed to him to such an extent that, where there would be no offence to his Divine Majesty and no imputation of sin to the neighbour, they desire to suffer injuries, false accusations, and to be held and esteemed as fools (but without their giving any occasion for this) because of their desire to resemble and imitate in some manner our Creator and Lord Jesus Christ. (General Examen 101)

Let us pray that you and I may begin to approach this high ideal.

Notes

Day 17: Conversion

For the last three days, you and I have been looking at and praying over the three considerations which constitute St Ignatius' build-up to making an election or choice about our life. They are the Two Standards, the Three Classes of People, and the Three Kinds or Degrees of Humility.

It might help to see how these are very much linked to each other and constitute a sort of development or progression.

> They can be summarized in terms of three elements: knowledge of Christ's way, commitment to Christ's way, and loving commitment to Christ's person. While each exercise is concerned with all three, the emphasis moves progressively from the first to the third. (Ivens, *Understanding the Spiritual Exercises*, p. 127)

The Two Standards is concerned above all with knowledge of the incompatibility between the way of Lucifer and the way of Christ, that God's ways are not our ways. And the prayer is to accept God's way even though it may include poverty and suffering.

In the Three Classes, the knowledge of the difference between them is taken for granted and the emphasis is on the condition necessary for sincere commitment, namely indifference in the Ignatian sense.

With the knowledge and commitment of the first

two exercises assumed, the emphasis in the Three Degrees of Humility is on the affective quality of love. 'This quality is, of course, present and effective throughout the whole sequence, but here it is carried to a new level of intensity and gratuitousness' (Ivens, p. 127).

This accords with what the Canadian theologian Bernard Lonergan says in his *Method in Theology* about conversion. He claims it can take place at three levels: intellectual, moral and religious. Each can happen independently from the other, though there is a natural tendency for each to relate to or lead on to the other.

Intellectual conversion is based on the knowledge of what is true and what is false. This is precisely what the meditation on the Two Standards is looking for as it compares the values of the world with the values of God's Kingdom.

Moral conversion is grounded in ethics, in the choice between good and evil. In other words, it is a matter for the will. The Three Classes of Persons illustrate where the will is inoperative, where it functions only at half strength, and where it is fully effective.

Religious conversion is, for Lonergan, the basis of the other two. He describes it as a radical opening to the person loved, without limits. It supposes letting oneself be captured by love and implies a total giving of oneself to the loved one, to Jesus Christ.

The Three Kinds of Humility leads up to this total giving. It is no longer a question of our understanding or our will but of our affections, our hearts. We want to share as fully as possible in the life of Jesus because we love him.

These are the choices that should accompany and determine my reply to the call of Christ. It may seem a little artificial to organise them according to our intellects, wills and hearts though it may help us to see better what our motives are, and to strengthen them. But really it is all part of the same conversion or movement Ignatius wants us to experience before we begin deciding, with his help and guidance, what needs to be changed in our lives.

This is expressed admirably in a well-known prayer that I wish to offer you for your own reflection and prayer today. It is sometimes called the Confederate Soldier's prayer because it was apparently found in the clothes of a soldier lying dead on the battlefield. It is a good summary of some of the petitions we have been trying to make in the three exercises mentioned above and should nourish the frame of mind and heart we need to embark on the election.

> I asked God for strength, that I might achieve.
> I was made weak, that I might learn humbly to obey.
> I asked for health, that I might do greater things.
> I was given infirmity, that I might do better things.
> I asked for riches, that I might be happy.
> I was given poverty, that I might be wise.
> I asked for power that I might have the praise of men.
> I was given weakness, that I might feel the need of God.
> I asked for all things, that I might enjoy life.
> I was given life, that I might enjoy all things.
> I got nothing that I asked for but got everything I had hoped for.
> Almost despite myself, my unspoken prayers were answered.
> I am, among all people, most richly blessed.

Notes

Day 18: Preparing Election or Amendment

In the earlier part of this retreat we saw that its main purpose is to help you take a close look at your life and to see in which way it is moving. And if it is moving away from your ultimate goal, to change direction and get you back on the right track.

As we have already seen, for some this may require a major decision affecting and changing their future; but for many the major decisions have already been taken and what is required is more a change or adjustment in something not working well. It is you who will have to decide, in the light of the prayer you have made so far, which category you belong to and therefore what sort of election you need to make.

St Ignatius gives ample directions for both and it is these we have to look at and pray over now. They both require a process of personal conversion and growth, issuing in a new commitment to Christ. And this is what we have been asking God for all along: a reformation of our life in which we seek and find God in a new, more direct and conscious way.

St Ignatius prefaces his remarks on the election with a preamble and an introductory statement. This is what I suggest you look at and pray over today. The preamble makes one simple and fairly obvious point – obvious, because this is precisely what you have been praying about these last few days. 'The eye of our intention must be simple.' In other words, whatever our eventual choice might be, 'it must help us towards the end for which we have been created.' This consideration must always come first, otherwise we run the risk of making 'the end fit the means' rather than 'subordinate the means to the end'.

Ignatius gives a simple example. 'It often happens that people choose first of all to marry, which is a means, and secondly to serve God in married life, though the service of God is the end.' To act like this is not to go straight to God, but to want God 'to come straight to their own disordered attachments'. You may think this is splitting hairs, but the distinction is crucial, as was made so clear in the meditation on the Three Classes of People. And this, as we have already seen, is the basic meaning of Ignatian indifference.

He ends by summing it up as follows: 'To sum up, nothing ought to induce me either to adopt such means or to reject them except the sole service and praise of God Our Lord and the eternal salvation of my soul.'

The introductory statement discusses mainly the scope or range of the election and once again repeats the dispositions we need to have. St Ignatius makes four simple and straightforward points:

1. The matters about which we wish to make an election must be either good in themselves or morally indifferent. They cannot be bad or repugnant to God or the Church.

2. Some elections involve unchangeable choices, such as marriage or the priesthood. Others are changeable.

3. Once an unchangeable election has been made, there are no further grounds for election since it cannot be undone. If however it hasn't been made properly (that is, without disordered attachments), 'one should

repent and try to lead a good life within the election one has made.'

4. For a changeable election, once it has been well made, there is no reason for making it over again. It should be lived to the best of one's ability. But if it hasn't been made 'sincerely and in good order', the opportunity should be taken to make it properly

Both for a formal election and in deciding what changes are needed in my present life, it will be helpful to accompany Jesus on a typical day in his life, as recounted in Mark's gospel:

- Jesus gets up early and goes to a lonely place to pray (1:35)
- The disciples come looking for him (1:36–37)
- They tell him about their own mission activity (6:30)
- Jesus invites them to come away and be on their own (6:31–32)
- But the people follow and Jesus takes pity on them (6:33–34)
- They need something to eat (6:35–36)
- Jesus tells the disciples to give them what they have (6:37–39)
- He himself shares out the fish and bread (6:40–44)
- The disciples get in the boat and go ahead to Bethsaida (6:45)
- Jesus goes into the hills to pray (6:46–47)
- He sees the disciples tired and in difficulties because of high winds (6:48)
- He walks out to them over the water (6:49)
- They are frightened but he says 'Courage, it is I' (6:51)
- He gets in the boat and the winds dropped (6:51–52)

- As soon as they land, the people recognise him (6:53–54)
- They hurry to bring all their sick (6:55
- All who touch him are cured (6:56)

Notes

Day 19: Discernment: Consolation/Desolation

Both those making a formal election and those concerned more with changing something in their present lives, might be helped by considering what St Ignatius has to say about the discernment of spirits to which he devotes much attention in the Exercises. It is a vast and complex topic we can't deal with adequately here and it calls for the help of an experienced director. What follows are a few simple comments that may be of some help in your prayer.

Many people are put off prayer because they say either nothing happens or that it is just one long struggle against distractions which we invariably end up by losing. This may be true but we have to remember that prayer is something God does in us, not something we do. Our task is to take the necessary steps that will enable God to pray in us, such as retiring to a quiet place, giving the full time we have decided on, and trying to achieve not only outer but inner silence. The rest we leave to God.

Sometimes we will feel great devotion and God will seem very near to us. This is what Ignatius calls *consolation* and defines more precisely as

> any interior movement produced in the soul that leads her to become inflamed with the love of her Creator and Lord, and when, as a consequence, there is no created thing on the face of the earth that we can love in itself, but we love it only in the Creator of all things.

This includes the gift of tears and necessarily increases our faith, hope and charity – a useful criterion to judge how genuine it is.

However, at other times we feel as dry as a bone and that God is deliberately hiding from us or has abandoned us. This is what Ignatius calls *desolation*, which he defines as everything contrary to what is said about consolation. In other words, 'it is darkness and disturbance in the soul, attraction to what is low and of the earth, anxiety arising from various agitations and temptations'. This can lead a person away from God, unless an intense effort is made to resist the temptations of the enemy through our own natural powers and the help of God which remains with us always even though we may not clearly feel it.

St Ignatius gives several important pieces of advice we can only summarize briefly here:

1. Not to feel guilty about being in desolation unless we have brought it on by our own carelessness or laziness in preparing our prayer time and keeping to it.

2. In time of desolation, make no hasty or precipitate changes in resolutions or decisions.

3. See the desolation as a period of trial which can help us grow, even though we ask the Lord to remove it when he sees fit. It can 'test our quality and show how far we will go in God's service and praise, even without generous recompense in the form of consolations and overflowing graces'.

4. 'When in consolation one must consider how one will bear oneself in the desolation that will follow later, and gather renewed strength for that moment.'

5. 'Only God Our Lord gives consolation to the soul without preceding cause', that is, it does not depend

on any other idea, text, image, or memory but is gratuitous and impossible to induce.

6. 'But when there is a cause, consolation can be given by the good or bad angel, but these give consolation for opposite purposes; the good angel for the soul's profit, so that the person grows and rises from good to better, the bad angel for the contrary purpose, so as eventually to draw the person into his own evil intentions and wickedness.'

Hopefully the above will have brought you light and not darkness and will be of some help in your daily prayer. As already mentioned above, any problems or misunderstandings you may have can be usefully discussed with a well-informed friend or 'director'.

For today's prayer, a suggestion is that you simply read through slowly and with devotion the gospel of St Mark. It is the shortest of the four gospels and, in some ways, the most direct and compelling. It was probably the first of the three synoptics and was used by both Matthew and Luke. But don't feel under any obligation to finish it. Rather let yourself be led by the Spirit, pausing and contemplating a scene wherever you are moved to do so.

Notes

Day 20: Process of Assessment

St Ignatius suggests that the method he proposes for making an election can also be used by someone considering a reform in their lives. It is in fact a clear and straightforward process of assessment that could be used for coming to any decision irrespective of a retreat. It contains six simple points:

1. To call to mind the issue at stake and make sure we have all the relevant information needed to reach a decision.
2. To remind myself what is my objective or end. Note it is not the thing itself I am trying to come to a decision about because that, as we have already seen, would be putting wrong things first, the cart before the horse. My objective or end must be that for which I was created. I will accept or refuse the matter I am making a choice about only in so far as it helps or hinders the former.
3. To ask God's help 'to move my will and put into my mind what I ought to do with regard to the thing before me that will be most for his praise and glory'.
4. To use my reason to assess the advantages and benefits that would accrue to me if I accepted the matter as well as the disadvantages and dangers; then to reverse the process, assessing the advantages and disadvantages if I refused it, all the time 'solely for the praise of God Our Lord and the good of my soul'. Thus there

will be four columns of pros and cons: advantages/disadvantages in accepting: advantages/ disadvantages in not accepting.

5. Then look to see in which direction reason inclines more, so that the conclusion is reached 'according to the stronger inclination of the reason, and not according to the inclinations of sensuality'.

6. Finally, having reached a decision, 'the person who made it should turn with great diligence to prayer, coming before God Our Lord, and offering him this election, so that his Divine Majesty may be pleased to accept and confirm it, if it is to his greater service and praise'.

Ignatius also suggests a second method, not so much for making an election, but for testing one already made. It contains four rules and a note:

1. First Rule: 'The love which moves me and makes me choose something has to descend from above, from the love of God; so that the one who makes the choice should first sense interiorly that the love he or she has, greater or less, for the object chosen is solely for the sake of the Creator and Lord.'

2. Second Rule: What would I tell another person to do, desiring their full perfection? 'I should then do the same myself, and keep the rule which I lay down for another.'

3. Third Rule: If I were at the point of death, 'to consider what procedure and what norms I would then wish to have followed in making the present election. I should then make my decision taking entirely these as my rule.'

4. Fourth Rule: 'To look and consider my situation on

the Day of Judgement, and think how at that moment I would want to have chosen in the present matter.'

Note: Having followed the above-mentioned Rules, I will make my election and offer it to God in accordance with Point 6 of the First Way.

All this may seem unnecessarily complicated and even far-fetched. But if you follow the directions, they turn out to be quite simple and not all that different from methods we ourselves might employ in trying to come to a decision on any complex issue. They amount to weighing the pros and cons within a specific context.

Sometimes God's will may be abundantly clear to us and leave us little room for choice. The classic example is the conversion of St Paul, falling blinded on the way to Damascus (Acts 9:1–9). At other times God may give us light and knowledge to see clearly through the sort of consolation in prayer we were considering yesterday. But neither of these situations depends on us and we can't control them. It is far more likely we will be groping in the dark, full of hesitations and doubts since, as St Paul says, 'we are seeing a dim reflection in a mirror' (1 Corinthians 13:12). Our self-knowledge is always incomplete and often, though we don't realise it, biased. It is therefore all the more important not only to ask God's help in coming to whatever decision we do but also to offer it in confidence and trust that God will direct us. A useful prayer in this respect is Psalm 139, which emphasises that God knows us better than we know ourselves.

Yahweh, you examine me and know me,
you know if I am standing or sitting,
you read my thoughts from far away,
whether I walk or lie down, you are watching,
you know every detail of my conduct ...

You know me through and through,
from having watched my bones take shape
when I was being formed in secret,
knitted together in the limbo of the womb.

You had scrutinised my every action,
all were recorded in your book,
my days listed and determined,
even before the first of them occurred ...

God, examine me and know my heart,
probe me and know my thoughts;
make sure I do not follow pernicious ways,
and guide me in the way that is everlasting.

Notes

Day 21: Offering and Confirmation

In the ways for making an election we looked at yesterday, as well as the procedure for amending and reforming our personal life, St Ignatius always ends by saying that we should come before God in prayer and offer our election or resolution to him, 'so that his Divine Majesty may be pleased to accept and confirm it, if it is to his greater service and praise'.

This is what I suggest for your prayer today. That you end this process by offering it to God in faith and hope and with great confidence.

Ignatius doesn't indicate how we may be certain that God will confirm it, but one sure sign would be an apostolically successful outcome, producing good results and being effective. Another could be feeling some degree of interior consolation from the fact we have taken a step to bring us nearer to God and his love for us.

But we know and must openly acknowledge that God's blessing and confirmation is essential. Psalm 127 will not let us forget this:

> If Yahweh does not build the house,
>   in vain the masons toil;
> If Yahweh does not guard the city,
>   in vain the sentries watch.
>
> In vain you get up earlier,
> and put off going to bed,

sweating to make a living,
since he provides for his beloved as they sleep.

A meditation or contemplation Ignatius suggests that might help us to make our formal dedication and offering, is the baptism of Our Lord in the Jordan. This marked the end of his private or hidden life and the beginning of his public life to set out on his Father's mission of proclaiming the message of love and salvation for all.

As always, we begin by asking for what we want. Here it is that God accept and confirm the offering we wish to make so that our lives in the future may be more open to God and more open to the needs of others.

The three simple points are based on the narrative in Matthew 3:13–17:

First. Christ Our Lord, having said farewell to his blessed mother, came from Nazareth to the river Jordan, where John the Baptist was.

Second. St John baptized Christ Our Lord, and when he wanted to excuse himself, judging that he was unworthy to baptize Christ, the latter said to him: 'Do this on the present occasion, because it is necessary for us to fulfil in this way all that is just.'

Third. The Holy Spirit came and the voice of the Father from heaven asserting: 'This is my beloved son with whom I am very satisfied.'

Jesus was very much aware he was setting out on the mission entrusted to him by his Father. It was not his own work but his Father's work. As he said more than once, it was to do his Father's will that he had come into the world. This is why the formal acceptance by his Father at his baptism is so significant. He is being missioned and his wish to receive John's baptism, which he did not need, is the visible sign of his formal acceptance of that mission.

You too, after this retreat, will be setting out on a new mission, or perhaps rather a mission that has been renewed. And you should want not only God's blessing and approval, but also God's presence and action in all that you do. For it is in this way that, however weak or insignificant we may be in ourselves, God can do great things through us.

The efficacy of my work for the Kingdom depends entirely on the degree to which God is able to work through me. Thus it depends on my determination to open myself to God and let God enter my life. As John the Baptist put it so succinctly: 'He must grow greater, I must grow less' (John 3:30).

The election or resolutions you have made under his guidance are precisely to facilitate this process and that is why you are offering them to God. May the Father say to you also: 'This is my beloved son/daughter in whom I am well pleased: listen to him/her.'

St Ignatius ends the second week of the Exercises with a short statement that sums up all he has been saying and amounts to a Golden Rule for life in the Spirit, recalling what we were looking at at the opening of this retreat: 'It must be borne in mind that a person will make progress in things of the spirit to the degree which they divest themselves of self-love, self-will, and self-interest.'

Notes

Day 22: The Passion

Today we begin the *Third Week of the Exercises* which is devoted to contemplation and prayer on Our Lord's Passion. We spent ten days on the First Week and eleven days on the Second Week. On the Third Week we will probably spend four days, and another four or five on the Fourth or final Week, devoted to Our Lord's Resurrection.

The shorter time for the last two weeks does not mean either that they are unimportant or that they are mere appendices or epilogues to the Exercises as a whole.

To some extent it is true that, if you have already made your election or resolutions for the amendment of your life, then the main work of the retreat has been completed. The contemplations on the Passion and Resurrection are to confirm you in your decisions and give you greater strength to carry them out.

But they also have an important value in themselves since they should help you to understand far more clearly what Our Lord's redemption consisted in and motivate you to co-operate with it more closely.

It is also important to bear in mind that, though the Passion and Resurrection are considered apart and placed in different Weeks, they really go together and should not be separated. They are both part of the same redemptive act, and one cannot be understood without the other.

In contemplating and praying over Our Lord's Passion, the fundamental grace we are asking for is 'compassion', which literally means 'suffering with'. This consists in an effort to relive what Our Lord himself went through, to experience it in ourselves. Many people find this very difficult and you may well be one of them.

For St Ignatius is attempting to move our feelings. He instructs us to ask for 'grief, deep feeling and confusion because it is for my sins that the Lord is going to his Passion'. And again we are to ask for 'grief with Christ in grief, to be broken with Christ broken, for tears and interior suffering on account of the great suffering that Christ endured for me'.

You may have to make these petitions in faith since it could well be that you experience no feeling at all, and certainly not 'tears and interior suffering'. You should not, however, be worried about this. We are often not masters of our own feelings and have already seen that it is God himself who gives 'consolation', when, how and to whom God chooses. We can also accept the fact that desolation and aridity may be the ways in which Jesus wants us to accompany him in his Passion.

Your task is to make the effort, trying to be present at whatever scene of the Passion calls your attention, and then to react to it in whichever way the Spirit moves you.

The first contemplation proposed by Ignatius is that of Our Lord's journey from Bethany to Jerusalem with his apostles and the Last Supper he shared with them. In St John's gospel, the Last Supper occupies no less than five lengthy chapters, so there is ample material for reflection and prayer.

The three preludes are the usual ones, recalling the history, seeing the place, and asking for what we desire. Here it will be 'grief, deep feeling and confusion because it is for my sins that the Lord is going to his Passion'.

St Ignatius also suggests three further considerations

that should accompany any meditation or contemplation on the Passion:

1. 'To consider what Christ Our Lord suffers in his human nature or wants to suffer'. This to arouse a feeling of love in return.
2. 'To consider how the divine nature goes into hiding, that is to say, how Christ, as divine, does not destroy his enemies, although he could do so, but allows himself in his sacred human nature to suffer most cruelly'.
3. 'To consider how he suffers all this for my sins, and what I myself ought to do and suffer for him'.

Ignatius puts special emphasis on the betrayal of Jesus by Judas after the washing of the feet, including those of Judas. But perhaps a good way of entering into this contemplation would be for you to read very slowly the account in St John (Chapters 13 – 17), stopping wherever you feel the inclination to do so without attempting to finish it all.

Notes

Day 23: Agony in the Garden

St Ignatius was a man of his time and placed much more emphasis than we probably would nowadays on the purely physical sufferings of Our Lord, as real and horrific as these were. This was precisely what Mel Gibson's film *The Passion of the Christ* set out to do, and was one of the reasons many felt put off by it. Yet, as Pope John Paul II is meant to have remarked after seeing it, 'This is how it happened.'

I don't know how you feel about this and you will have to make up your own mind to what extent you dwell on this aspect of the Passion. Though I have to admit it is a source of continual surprise to me how people tend to shy away from physical considerations in our modern world when the use of torture and violence is so widespread and systematic. One only has to read the annual reports of Amnesty International or the International Helsinki Federation on Human Rights to realise how true this is.

Clearly the above also applies to mental torture equally widely and deliberately used. And it leads us into the second contemplation on the Passion, proposed by St Ignatius, the Agony in the Garden. (See Matthew 26:30–56; Mark 14:26–52; Luke 22:31–53.)

The prayer for what we desire is more explicit that the previous one of yesterday: 'To ask for grief with Christ in grief, to be broken with Christ broken, for tears and interior suffering on account of the great suffering Christ endured for me'.

Ignatius does not propose points for this contemplation, but in recalling its history emphasises the three incidents to which we should pay attention:

1. First of all, there is Our Lord's agony in the garden. 'A sudden fear came over him and great distress. And he said to them, "My soul is sorrowful to the point of death. Wait here and keep awake with me." And going on a little further he threw himself on the ground and prayed that, if it were possible, this hour might pass him by. "Abba (Father)!" he said. "Everything is possible for you. Take this cup away from me. But let it be as you, not I, would have it." This prayer he repeated three times, adding 'Let your will be done, not mine'. And Luke adds: 'In his anguish he prayed even more earnestly, and his sweat fell to the ground like great drops of blood.'

It is impossible for us to know exactly what Our Lord's agony consisted in. It must certainly have included the foreknowledge of the sufferings he was about to undergo, both at the hands of the Jews and Roman soldiers and on the Cross itself. Did it also include the sensation of being abandoned by his Father which he experienced on the Cross? If so, it might have included doubts as to whether it was all worthwhile in the light of his redemption being rejected by so many millions in the course of human history.

These considerations may help us when we feel abandoned or that life is useless. We can draw some comfort from the fact that Jesus Christ has been there before us.

2. Secondly there is the behaviour of the Apostles. It

starts with Peter's declaration: 'Even if all lose faith, I will not . . . If I have to die with you, I will never disown you.' Both Mark and Matthew add: 'And they all said the same.' Our Lord's reply is only too familiar: 'I tell you solemnly, this day, this very night, before the cock crows twice, you will have disowned me three times.' And then in the garden he asks the three he took in with him: 'Wait here and keep awake. Pray not to be put to the test.' Yet three times he returned to find them asleep.

How would you or I have behaved? Would we too have made false promises? Would we have slept as well? Let us consider the many times we have paid little or no attention to the Lord's word. And let us ask him to forgive us.

3. The final scene is Our Lord's arrest in the garden. It starts with Judas coming in with a number of armed men and kissing Jesus to identify him. Jesus said to him: 'Judas, are you betraying the Son of Man with a kiss?' Then one of the bystanders drew his sword and struck out at the high priest's servant, and cut off his ear. Jesus immediately healed him and told them to put their swords away. Then he added: 'Am I a brigand that you had to set out with swords and clubs? When I was among you in the Temple day after day you never moved to lay hands on me. But this is your hour; this is the reign of darkness.' As for the apostles, 'they all deserted him and ran away'. Mark adds: 'A young man who followed him had nothing on but a linen cloth. They caught hold of him, but he left the cloth in their hands and ran away naked.' Many think this was Mark himself.

Once again we can reflect on our behaviour, had we been present. How many times have you and I betrayed the Lord, either directly by something we have done or just by running away? Once again we ask for his forgiveness.

As usual, the contemplation should end with a colloquy (or conversation) with Our Lord or, as Ignatius adds: 'If the matter or a particular devotion moves me, I can make three colloquies, one to the Mother, one to the Son, one to the Father.'

Notes

Day 24: Treatment by Jews and Romans

One of the ways of meditating or contemplating on the Passion for those who find it difficult, is to look at it through someone else's eyes. For example, through the eyes of Mary, Peter, John, the Roman centurion, or even Pilate. This may be a help in appreciating different aspects of it.

But its fundamental mystery remains. Why was it necessary? God could have so easily redeemed mankind in a different or even painless way. Why didn't God do it?

It is no more possible to answer this question than it is to understand why there is so much suffering by totally innocent people. Why, to use the technical term, does the problem of evil exist?

We have already seen that the cause of so much injustice and suffering in the world is due to sin, to the refusal of human beings to accept God's invitation to love and build a civilisation based on love.

But why is it the innocent who seem to suffer most? Why are there so many children being exploited, abused, forced to work as slaves? I lived and worked in El Salvador during its civil war and saw so many heart-rending examples of totally blameless people being tortured and massacred. The six Jesuits, their housekeeper and her daughter who were assassinated by the army on our university campus were all good friends of mine. It was impossible not to ask why. I am sure you too have had similar experiences.

It was the French poet Claudel who said: 'Jesus didn't come to explain suffering, but to fill it with his presence.'

This was understood very well by Archbishop Oscar Romero of El Salvador who was himself martyred because he stood for justice and the rights of the poor. He realised perfectly well that, if the Church were true to its mission, it would receive the same treatment as Jesus himself received and that he promised to his apostles. Opposition and persecution were inevitable.

He actually said: 'A church that suffers no persecution but enjoys the privileges and support of the things of the earth – beware – it is not the true church of Jesus Christ.'

And he added: 'I am glad, brothers and sisters, that our church is persecuted precisely for its preferential option for the poor.' He was able to rejoice that priests and religious were being killed alongside workers and peasants since it was a sign of authenticity, of God's blessing.

None of this is a logical explanation of the cross or innocent suffering but it was St Paul himself who said we cannot and should not expect this.

> Christ did not send me to baptise, but to preach the Good News, and not to preach that in the terms of philosophy in which the crucifixion of Christ cannot be expressed. The language of the cross may be illogical to those who are not on the way to salvation, but those of us who are on the way see it as God's power to save. (1 Corinthians 1:17–19)

I hope this will help you, not to solve the mystery, but to understand better how 'God's foolishness is wiser than human wisdom, and God's weakness is stronger than human strength' (1 Corinthians 1:25).

The contemplation proposed by Ignatius takes us from the arrest of Jesus to his carrying the cross to Calvary. Though the story may be well known and familiar to you, it is worth listing the main events and inviting you to choose and rest with whichever attracts you most. Here is the list identified by Ignatius:

1. Jesus was taken bound first to the house of Annas where Peter denied him for the first time.
2. Then he was taken to the house of Caiaphas, the high priest, who questioned him and whose servant slapped him in the face for his reply. Peter denied him twice more and the cock crew. During the night, those holding Jesus mocked him, beat him, blindfolded him and struck him blows in the face, asking 'Prophesy to us! Who has struck you?'
3. He was then taken before Pilate to whom the Jews accused him of perverting the people and forbidding the paying of tribute to Caesar. Pilate examined him and asked him if he was king of the Jews. When Jesus said he had come into the world to bear witness to the truth, Pilate said: 'Truth? What is that?' He then said: 'I find no case against him.' He offered to release Barabbas, a thief, or Jesus, but the crowd shouted for Barabbas.
4. Pilate sent Jesus, the Galilean, to Herod, tetrarch of Galilee, who questioned him at length. Jesus refused to reply, so they dressed him in a white garment and mocked him. Herod sent him back to Pilate and the two men became friends after having been enemies.
5. Pilate took Jesus and had him flogged; and the soldiers made a crown of thorns and they put it on his head, and they clothed him in purple and came up to

him saying 'Hail, King of the Jews', and they struck him blows in the face.

6. Pilate then presented him to the Jews, dressed in a purple robe and crowned with thorns: 'Here is the man.' They shouted: 'Crucify him! Crucify him!' Pilate was frightened and wanted to set him free, but the Jews insisted and in the end he handed him over to them to be crucified.

7. Jesus started on the way to Calvary but was too weak to carry the cross and had to be helped by Simon of Cyrene.

Notes

Day 25: Seven Last Words on the Cross

The final contemplation of the Third Week is devoted to Our Lord's death on the cross, though St Ignatius also admits a contemplation on the Passion as a whole.

A traditional way of contemplating the crucifixion is to reflect on and hear Our Lord's seven last words. Ignatius lists them as follows:

1. 'Father, forgive them: they do not know what they are doing.' Then they cast lots to share out his clothing. These words were spoken after Jesus had been nailed to the cross and in the midst of jeers and mockery by the bystanders. 'He saved others. Let him save himself if he is the Christ of God, the Chosen One.' The soldiers mocked him too and said: 'If you are the King of the Jews, save yourself' (Luke 23:34–37).

2. 'One of the criminals hanging there abused him. "Are you not the Christ?" he said. "Save yourself and us as well." But the other spoke up and rebuked him. "Have you no fear of God at all?" he said. "You got the same sentence as he did, but in our case we deserved it: we are paying for what we did. But this man has done nothing wrong. Jesus," he said, "remember me when you come into your kingdom." "Indeed I promise you," he replied "today you will be with me in paradise"' (Luke 23:39–43).

3. 'Near the cross of Jesus stood his mother and his mother's sister, Mary the wife of Clopas, and Mary of

Magdala. Seeing his mother and the disciple he loved standing near her, Jesus said to his mother, "Woman, this is your son." Then to the disciple he said, "This is your mother." And from that moment the disciple made a place for her in his home' (John 19:25–27).

4. 'After this, Jesus knew that everything had now been completed, and to fulfil the scripture perfectly he said: "I am thirsty." A jar full of vinegar stood there, so putting a sponge soaked in the vinegar on a hyssop stick they held it up to his mouth' (John 19:28–29).

5. 'From the sixth hour there was darkness over all the land until the ninth hour. At about the ninth hour, Jesus cried out in a loud voice, "*Eli, Eli, lama sabachthani?*" that is, "*My God, my God, why have you deserted me?*" When some of those who stood there heard this, they said, "The man is calling on Elijah" ... "Wait!" said the rest of them "and see if Elijah will come to save him"' (Matthew 27:45–49).

6. 'When Jesus had cried out in a loud voice, he said, "Father, into your hands I commend my spirit"' (Luke 23:46).

7. 'But Jesus, again crying out in a loud voice, yielded up his spirit. At that, the veil of the Temple was torn in two from top to bottom; the earth quaked; the rocks were split; the tombs opened and the bodies of many holy men rose from the dead, and these, after his resurrection, came out of the tombs, entered the Holy City and appeared to a number of people' (Matthew 27:50–53). When the centurion saw what had taken place, he gave praise to God and said, "This was a great and good man." And when all the people who had gathered for the spectacle saw what had happened, they went home beating their breasts' (Luke 22:47–48).

In human terms the cross means total disgrace and failure. But in Christian terms, as St Paul so often declared, it becomes the sign of victory over death, of new life, of success.

> And so, while the Jews demand miracles and the Greeks look for wisdom, here are we preaching a crucified Christ; to the Jews an obstacle they cannot get over, to the pagans madness, but to those who have been called, whether they are Jews or Greeks, a Christ who is the power and wisdom of God. (1 Corinthians 1:23–24)

This became a key point in Paul's preaching. 'During my stay with you, the only knowledge I claimed to have was about Jesus, and only about him as the crucified Christ' (1 Corinthians 2:2). 'As for me, the only thing I can boast about is the cross of our Lord Jesus Christ, through whom the world is crucified to me, and I to the world' (Galatians 6:14). This is his message to you and me. Can we say with Paul: 'I have been crucified with Christ, and I live now not with my own life but with the life of Christ who lives in me'? (Galatians 2:20).

The above should not be considered in a wholly personal manner as if referring to me alone. We need also to be aware of the presence of the mystery of death and resurrection in the world around us today: in the suffering and death of millions of people brought about by poverty, by war and by unjust and oppressive social structures and systems; and in the coming-to-life that takes place by the power of God even in the midst of such evils. Christ is dying and being raised from the dead daily all round us in his sisters and brothers.

Perhaps the last word can be left to St John who, in

his gospel, quotes Jesus meditating on his future Passion and explaining its deepest meaning (John 12:23–32):

'Now the hour has come for the Son of Man to be glorified. I tell you most solemnly, unless a wheat grain falls on the ground and dies, it remains only a single grain; but if it dies, it yields a rich harvest. Anyone who loves his life loses it; anyone who hates his life in this world will keep it for the eternal life. If a man serves me, he must follow me, wherever I am, my servant will be there too. If anyone serves me, my Father will honour him. Now my soul is troubled. What shall I say: Father, save me from this hour? But it was for this very reason that I have come to this hour. Father, glorify your name . . . Now sentence is being passed on this world; now the prince of this world is to be overthrown. And when I am lifted up from the earth, I shall draw all men to myself.'

A prayerful reflection on this passage may help you to see the crucifixion in its true light.

Notes

Day 26: The Resurrection

The *Fourth and final Week of the Exercises* is devoted to Our Lord's Resurrection, without which his Passion makes no sense. St Paul was very clear on this, as he told the Corinthians: 'If Christ has not been raised then our preaching is useless and your believing it is useless . . . If our hope in Christ has been for this life only, we are the most unfortunate of all people' (1 Corinthians 15:14 and 19).

The overriding sentiment we are asked to experience in this Week is one of joy. As Ignatius puts it, 'ask for the grace to feel gladness and to rejoice intensely over the great glory and joy of Christ Our Lord'.

Once again, as with sadness, this joy is a gift of the Spirit which the retreatant can't conjure up at will. We may well not experience huge consolation or tears, but we should at least find a certain peace and tranquillity because the Lord has conquered death and his victory is ours too.

A certain joy should in any case always be a natural disposition of any Christian because, as Pope John Paul II put it so well, 'We are an Easter People and Alleluia is our song.'

Religious faith is sometimes portrayed as something negative, inducing gloom. Some of our church services doubtless create such an impression. But this is quite wrong. We should pay more attention to St Paul's advice: 'Be happy at all times' (1 Thessalonians 5:16).

Why? The answer comes from Psalm 126:

> Then our mouths filled with laughter
> and our lips with song.
> Even the pagans started talking
> about the marvels Yahweh had done for us!
> What marvels indeed he did for us,
> and how overjoyed we were!
>
> (Psalm 126:2–3)

In the Exercises for the Fourth Week, Ignatius suggests only one contemplation and uniquely for him, it is a scene we don't find in the gospels. It is the appearance of Jesus Christ to his mother. Widespread devotion holds that it did take place and what we ask is to share in the joy of a mother who learns that her son is not dead but alive, that 'the loneliness of Our Lady with her grief and exhaustion' have been transformed.

In your prayer you can take this scene or use any of the other apparitions of Jesus as recounted in the gospel. For example, there are:

1. The race between Peter and John to get to the tomb early on Easter Sunday morning with John arriving first because he ran faster. On entering, they saw the linen cloths on the ground and the one that had been over his head rolled up in a place by itself. Our Lord didn't appear to them, but they saw and believed. 'Till this moment they had failed to understand the teaching of scripture, that he must rise from the dead' (John 20:1–10).

2. Our Lord's appearance in the garden to Mary Magdalene, who at first didn't recognise Jesus and thought he was the gardener. "'Sir, if you have taken him away, tell me where you have put him, and I will go and remove him." Jesus said, "Mary!" She knew him then

and said to him in Hebrew, "Rabbuni!" – which means Master. Jesus said to her, "Do not cling to me, because I have not yet ascended to the Father. But go and find the brothers, and tell them I am ascending to my Father, to my God and your God'" (John 20:11–18).

3. The appearance of Jesus to the twelve, first without Thomas, then the following week with him. 'He said to them, "Peace be with you" and showed them his hands and his side. The disciples were filled with joy when they saw the Lord . . . Thomas was not with them when Jesus came . . . He answered, "Unless I see the holes that the nails made in his hands and can put my finger into the holes they made, and unless I can put my hand into his side, I refuse to believe" . . . Then he spoke to Thomas, "Put your finger here; look, here are my hands. Give me your hand; put it into my side. Doubt no longer but believe." Thomas replied, "My Lord and my God!" Jesus said to him: "You believe because you can see me. Happy are those who have not seen yet believe"' (John 20:19–29).

4. The appearance to the two disciples walking to Emmaus. At first they didn't recognise him, but he asked them why they were so sad and what they were discussing. They told him and 'he said to them, "You foolish men! So slow to believe the full message of the prophets! Was it not ordained that the Christ should suffer and so enter his glory?" Then starting with Moses and going through all the prophets, he explained to them the passages throughout the scriptures that were about himself.' He went in to stay with them and they recognised him in the breaking of the bread. 'Then they said to each other, "Did not our hearts burn within us as he talked to us on the

road and explained the scriptures to us?"They set out
that instant and returned to Jerusalem' (Luke 24:13–
35).

These apparitions have some elements in common that
are worth noting:

1. In a first moment, Jesus is not recognised. Only after
    a time, sometimes long, is it realised it is him. How
    often are we the same?
2. Jesus met the people exactly where they were. With
    the exception of Mary Magdalene, he was looking
    for them and not they for him.
3. His appearance was a totally unexpected surprise.
4. In all it produced an immediate and dramatic effect,
    a change of life.

In contemplating these scenes, I suggest your prayer be one
above all of presence, of just being there in silence, without
many thoughts or words. In this way you will share in the
joy of the people to whom Our Lord appeared.

Notes

Day 27: By the Sea of Galilee

For today's prayer, I want to suggest the wonderful last chapter of St John's gospel which recounts in detail Our Lord's final appearance to his apostles on the shore of the sea of Galilee where he had first met so many of them.

The chapter (21) comes after the formal conclusion of John's gospel which leads the experts to believe it was added as an afterthought, either by John himself or a disciple, as a sort of appendix.

Our prayer is the same as yesterday: 'ask for the grace to feel gladness and to rejoice intensely over the great glory and joy of Christ Our Lord'.

The chapter raises a number of issues that can be reduced to the following seven:

1. 'I'm going fishing': Our Lord had told the apostles to go up to Galilee and wait for him there. While still in Jerusalem they had already been empowered by Jesus to forgive sins and, though not yet Pentecost, had received at least in part the gift of the Holy Spirit. But they don't seem to have realised yet what this involved and didn't seem to know what to do. From the gospel text they appear bored, so when Peter said 'I'm going fishing', the others replied immediately 'We'll come with you'. So they went out and spent all night fishing but caught nothing.

2. 'Throw the net out to starboard and you'll find something': When dawn came, Jesus stood on the shore but the apostles didn't recognise him. He asked

if they had caught anything and then told them to throw out the net on the other side. The result was a huge haul of fish so great that they could not haul it in. The lesson is clear and applies not only to you and me, but to the church as a whole. When we are doing our own thing in our own way, we often fail or achieve minimal results. But, if instead of relying on ourselves, we follow the Lord's instructions and do it his way, the results can be overwhelming.

3. 'It is the Lord': At this moment, John recognises Jesus and says 'It is the Lord'. Peter, wearing very little, threw his cloak around him and jumped into the water. The others followed in the boat, towing the net and the fish. It probably takes you and me some time to recognise Jesus. We often don't see him at first in a particular event or happening, and may need someone else to point him out. But when we do recognise him, do we welcome him with joy and excitement like Peter?

4. 'Come and have breakfast': Our Lord tells the apostles to bring some of the fish and come and eat. They had apparently already counted the fish, possibly to share them out, and arrived at the number of 153. They didn't dare ask him who he was because 'they knew quite well it was the Lord'. Jesus then shared some fish with them and 'took the bread and gave it to them'. It is not clear whether this meal constituted a Eucharist, as with the two disciples on the way to Emmaus, or whether the apostles finally recognised him 'in the breaking of the bread'. What is clear is that the Lord seems to have cooked and prepared the meal himself and thus shows the care he takes for our ordinary needs, if we place our trust in him. Many ingenious suggestions have been made to explain the number 153, but these needn't occupy us here.

5. 'Simon, son of John, do you love me?': Jesus asked Peter this question three times which upset him, so he finally replied: 'Lord, you know everything: you know I love you.' Jesus said to him, 'Feed my sheep.' I have always thought Our Lord asked Peter three times because Peter had denied him three times. Can we make Peter's final answer? If not, let us ask God to help us. Note that the important mission Jesus gave to Peter depended on his capacity to love.

6. 'When you grow old': Jesus then tells Peter that, in his old age, things will be done to him he will not like and that others will have control. But he then says: 'Follow me.' Whatever your age, which I don't know, this is an opportunity for us to consider old age and death, not as purely negative and destructive things, but rather as an invitation to follow Jesus more closely and thus enter into his life. Though perhaps in human terms at times painful and unpleasant, they are necessary paths to the fuller and more complete life that awaits us all.

7. 'What about him, Lord?': Having been told about his own future, Peter then asks Jesus what will happen to John. Jesus replies: 'What does it matter to you? You are to follow me.' I sometimes wonder if Peter was jealous of the disciple whom Jesus loved. We are often jealous of others. Can we accept the advice Jesus gave to Peter to get on with our own business, and leave the fate of others to him?

Notes

Day 28: Pentecost

Physically Our Lord's mission ended with his ascension into heaven and his handing over to the apostles, commissioning them to go and make disciples of all nations, baptising 'them in the name of the Father and of the Son and of the Holy Spirit, and teach them to observe all the commands I gave you'. But just as he left them, his final words were: 'Know that I am with you always: yes, to the end of time' (Matthew 28:19–20).

At the Last Supper, he explained to his apostles that he was not leaving them 'orphans'. He had to go so that the Holy Spirit could come who 'will teach you everything and remind you of all I have said to you' (John 14:18, 26).

So it is more accurate to say Our Lord's mission only really ended with the coming of the Holy Spirit which, for this reason, marks the birthday of the church. Therefore, before ending this Fourth Week of the Exercises, it is important to consider the fact of Pentecost even though St Ignatius doesn't devote a contemplation to this theme. This is what I wish to propose to you today.

Your prayer should be that the Holy Spirit will come into your heart and into the hearts of all the members of his church. 'Come, Holy Spirit, fill the hearts of your faithful, and kindle in them the fire of your love.'

The reflection or contemplation is on Luke's account of Pentecost (Acts 2:1–47):

1. 'They had all met in one room': very possibly the same room in which Jesus appeared to them, in

which case the doors and windows were barred 'for fear of the Jews'.

2. But the Spirit burst in, like a powerful wind from heaven, and settled on the heads of each 'like tongues of fire'. 'They were all filled with the Holy Spirit, and began to speak foreign languages as the Spirit gave them the gift of speech.'

3. Windows and doors were opened immediately and they started preaching to the crowds

4. The people were amazed and astonished. 'Surely' they said 'all these men speaking are Galileans? How does it happen that each of us hears him in his own native language?'

5. Peter stood up and addressed the crowd in a loud voice. The first thing he had to establish was that they were not drunk. Their speaking in tongues was the effect of the Holy Spirit, as was foretold by the prophets. Then he went on to claim that Jesus of Nazareth was a man commended to them by God by the miracles and signs he worked, but whom 'you took and had crucified by men outside the Law. You killed him, but God raised him to life . . . God raised this man Jesus to life, and all of us are witnesses to that.'

6. 'Hearing this, they were cut to the heart and said to Peter and the apostles "What must we do, brothers?" "You must repent", Peter answered, "and every one of you must be baptised in the name of Jesus Christ for the forgiveness of your sins, and you will receive the gift of the Holy Spirit."'

7. 'He spoke to them for a long time using many arguments, and he urged them, 'Save yourselves from this perverse generation.' They were convinced by his arguments, and they accepted what he said and were

baptised. That very day about three thousand were added to their number.'

So was the church born and so it grew. The whole of the Acts of the Apostles is full of examples of the effect of the Spirit on the early Christians. Before receiving it, the apostles themselves were simple, ignorant fishermen, scared of the Jews. After it they became fearless preachers of the Good News, travelling all over the known world, not afraid to speak out before great and wise men and often to suffer the consequences.

They were arrested by the Sanhedrin who wanted to put them to death. But a Pharisee called Gamaliel said: '"What I suggest is that you leave these men alone and let them go. If this enterprise, this movement of theirs, is of human origin it will break up of its own accord; but if it does in fact come from God you will not only be unable to destroy them but you might find yourself fighting against God." His advice was accepted; and they had the apostles called in, gave orders for them to be flogged, and warned them not to speak in the name of Jesus and released them. And so they left the presence of the Sanhedrin glad to have had the honour of suffering humiliation for the sake of the name' (Acts 5:38–41).

Perhaps in making your final prayer to the Spirit, you can again offer your election or resolutions, asking the Spirit to confirm them and give you the strength and courage to live them.

Notes

Day 29: Contemplation to Attain Love

We began this retreat by considering that we were created by love in order to love, that our fundamental purpose or aim in life is to move from the selfish love with which we are all born to a totally unselfish love that is our only way of sharing in the existence of God who is love.

We end the retreat by returning to a consideration of love in the final contemplation proposed by St Ignatius, known as the Contemplation to Attain Love.

It doesn't add anything new to what we have already seen, but it does confirm it and make it more explicit, summing up what has been present since the beginning and throughout the Exercises.

The grace we ask for is a double one: to realise how gifted we are, surrounded on all sides by love and, in the gratitude this arouses, to respond by loving and serving God in all things. In the words of Ignatius: 'To ask for interior knowledge of all the good I have received, so that acknowledging this with gratitude, I may be able to love and serve his Divine Majesty in everything.'

The contemplation begins with two brief notes. 'First: love ought to find its expression in deeds rather than in words.' We should be concerned with actions, not promises. 'Second: love consists in mutual communication. That is to say, the lover gives and communicates to the loved one what they have, or something of what they have, or are able to give; and in turn the one loved does the same for the lover.'

The contemplation is developed in four points, each of which covers an area of human reality and illustrates a mode of God's loving presence and action. We are invited to reflect on our personal history, on the material world which is our environment, and on our personal qualities. And we encounter God through God's gifts: *bestowing* them, *present* in them, *working* in them, and *source* of them.

The four points, with one leading naturally to the other, are as follows:

1. *Bestowing them*: Consider all the benefits or gifts God has given you: your creation, your redemption, and all the other particular gifts you have. Then reflect within yourself what you ought to offer back to God. It is here that St Ignatius introduces his famous prayer of offering which should be repeated 'with much affection' after each point in the contemplation and can be used outside the Exercises in our daily prayers:

   Take Lord and receive all my liberty, my memory, my understanding and my entire will, all that I have and possess. You gave it all to me; to you I return it. All is yours, dispose of it entirely according to your will. Give me only the love of you, together with your grace for that is enough for me.

2. *Present in them*: The second point is to see how God dwells in all creatures: in the elements, plants, animals and humankind, and therefore in you, giving you being, life, and sensation and causing you to understand. And again to reflect within yourself what return you should make.

3. *Working in them*: God is not only present in his gifts,

but is actually working and labouring on your behalf
in all the created things on the face of the earth. Then
to reflect within yourself. Here would enter the
consideration of how we use these things and what
we prayed about earlier on in connection with the
problem of global warming which is destroying God's
earth.

4. *Source of them*: To see how all that is good in this world
    descends from on high. This takes you beyond your
    own personal life to consider the source of all the
    good things you can imagine. Then to finish by
    reflecting within yourself.

Your final prayer should take up again the offering
suggested by St Ignatius, requesting the help of Mary, Jesus
and the Father to make it honestly and effectively. It is an
offering of yourself, made in love, to God who, because
of love for you, has given you so much. In this offering,
include the resolutions of this retreat.

Notes

Day 30: Prayer in Daily Life

Congratulations! You have reached the last day of this retreat! At the end of a retreat, the main problem often faced by the retreatant is how to pass what has been learnt and experienced into one's ordinary daily life without losing it.

In this, prayer is likely to be the crucial factor. During the retreat you have been able to devote a specific time each day to God. This has entailed finding a suitable place free of interruptions and observing silence. It may well be impossible to continue doing this on resuming your normal life.

However, I believe it is essential you make the effort to see how you can devote at least some time to prayer each day. This is perhaps the reason why Ignatius ends the Exercises with instructions on 'Three Ways of Praying'. I am loath to enter into these here in any great detail since everyone prays in a different way and our real master in prayer has to be none other than God who will lead us surely if we allow this to happen.

But it is worth stressing one point that makes St Ignatius such an important master of the spiritual life even today. He put great emphasis on finding God in all things. As one modern writer on Ignatian spirituality has put it: 'For Ignatius the flurry of daily life is where we grow towards God. Activities like prayer, worship or contemplation clearly have an important place in this wider sense of spirituality as a way of living, but theirs is not necessarily the most important place.' Though Ignatius probably never used the expression himself, the hallmark of his spirituality is to be 'a contemplative in action'.

This doesn't mean we should abandon the effort to withdraw from things and seek God in the silence of our hearts. This is still necessary, even essential. But it does mean we should also seek God in the ordinary events of our lives, in relationships, in other people. It is a question of letting privileged moments speak more deeply, of dwelling on them, savouring them, entering into them as, in an Ignatian contemplation, we enter into a gospel scene and make ourselves present at it. The opportunities are infinite and as varied and complex as life itself.

It is not so much raising the mind and heart to God, up or out there or even hidden within, but rather discovering him/her present all the time in the essence of things, in others, in encounters, places, events, situations, even the most unlikely. These include, of course, suffering, pain, tears and anguish for the God of surprises is lurking there too, if only we will peel away the outer layers to uncover him/her. Child abuse, racial oppression, AIDS, torture of the innocent, exploitation of the poor, however abominable and worthy of condemnation in themselves, can all be occasions for discovering God's love and gentleness.

The three ways of praying identified by Ignatius are:

1. To take a particular text (Ten Commandments, Seven Deadly Sins, Three Powers of the Soul, etc.) and to go through it item by item and examining how I have kept or failed to keep it, and asking forgiveness and pardon where needed.
2. To take a particular prayer (Our Father, Hail Mary, Creed, Soul of Christ, etc.) and going through it word by word, stopping on finding 'rich matter for reflection and much relish and consolation'

3. Praying mentally with each intake or expulsion of breath, by saying one word of the Our Father or of any other prayer being said, so that only a single word is pronounced between one breath and the next.

These ways obviously require a fuller explanation as well as some practice, but the last 'by rhythm' suggests more the prayer of silence we were considering on Day 2 of the retreat. It emphasises we should try to let God pray within us. For it is not you or I who are praying, but God who is praying within us.

A practice that can help our daily prayer and is strongly recommended in the Exercises (cf. 24–31) is the daily 'examen' or examination of conscience. This is a brief time of prayer when we reflect on the day's events and try to discern in them the presence or absence of God. St Ignatius distinguishes five moments or 'points' in this prayer (cf. 43).

1. *Gratitude*: Give thanks to God for the benefits I have received, especially during this day.
2. *Petition*: I ask God for the grace to know my sins and reject them.
3. *Review*: To review my thoughts, words and deeds during this day, aware of God's presence or absence in them.
4. *Forgiveness*: Ask God to pardon what I have done wrong during the day.
5. *Amendment*: Look at the day ahead and plan amendment. Our Father.

In his own life, St Ignatius was a profound mystic and gave an outstanding example of God's presence and action in all that he did. This can be seen clearly from the entries in his Spiritual Diary (see Endnotes). I would like to leave the final word with him in a prayer sometimes attributed to him which in a way sums all we have done in this retreat:

> Lord,
> teach me to be generous.
> Teach me to love and serve you as you deserve;
> to give and not to count the cost;
> to fight and not to heed the wounds;
> to toil and not to seek for rest;
> to labour and to look for no reward
> save that of knowing
> that I am doing your most holy will.

Notes

Endnotes

1: If you want to get a good collection of the personal writings of St Ignatius, including the Spiritual Exercises, these have been published in a Penguin Classic called *Saint Ignatius of Loyola: Personal Writings*, which should be easy to obtain.

The Bible version used in this book is that of *The Jerusalem Bible*, copyright © 1966, 1967 and 1968 by Darton, Longman & Todd Ltd and Doubleday & Company, Inc.

This retreat is now available at: http://www.spirexnet.co.uk.

I hope this retreat has been of some use to you. I am well aware that it could and should be improved. If you have any corrections/suggestions to make or any other comments, I would be very happy to hear from you. I can be reached at sjbar@caribsurf.com.